NATIONAL GEOGRAPHIC KiDS

ANGRY BIRDS™
EXPLORE THE WORLD!

PACKED WITH ANIMALS, FUN FACTS, GAMES, MAPS, AND MORE!

NATIONAL GEOGRAPHIC
WASHINGTON, D.C.

Contents

WELCOME TO THE WORLD

THE ANGRY BIRDS AND NATIONAL GEOGRAPHIC TAKE OFF ON A FUN ADVENTURE.

Ready to explore the world? The Angry Birds sure are, and you're invited! National Geographic will take you on a one-of-a-kind adventure as you follow Red, Bomb, Chuck, and the Blues through seven continents. You'll meet bottlenose dolphins in North America, a giant panda in Asia, and a koala in Australia. Your itinerary also includes the coolest places on Earth—from Machu Picchu in Peru to the Pyramids at Giza in Egypt.

Come face-to-face with some of the world's most interesting cultures, such as the Maasai of Africa. And did you know that most fish in Antarctica have natural "antifreeze" in their blood? Weird-but-true facts such as these are packed in for the ride, along with funny observations from Red and the gang as they explore the world.

So zip up your suitcase and get ready to fly! The Angry Birds and National Geographic have planned the perfect adventure, just for you.

NAME RED
ALIAS RED BIRD
HOBBIES CHESS, PHYSICS
STRONGEST ALLY CHUCK

NAME THE BLUES
ALIAS THE BLUES
HOBBIES MUSIC, ACTING, DRAWING
STRONGEST ALLIES EACH OTHER

NORTH AMERICA
EUROPE
ASIA
SOUTH AMERICA
AFRICA
AUSTRALIA
ANTARCTICA

NAME BOMB
ALIAS BLACK BIRD
HOBBIES CALLIGRAPHY
STRONGEST ALLY RED

NAME CHUCK
ALIAS YELLOW BIRD
HOBBIES SPORTS
STRONGEST ALLY RED

WELCOME TO NORTH AMERICA

> YEE-HAW! WE'RE READY TO RIDE!

> 5,550 MILES? I'M ALREADY TIRED!

"AMERICA THE BEAUTIFUL" MAY HAVE BEEN WRITTEN ABOUT THE UNITED STATES, BUT

its words definitely describe the entire continent of North America. East to west, nearly 5,500 miles separate sea from shining sea, filled with ginormous mountains, plains that go on forever, snow-covered Arctic lands, sun-drenched deserts, and lush rain forests. With such diverse environments, no wonder everything from polar bears to jaguars to a crazy-looking bird called a quetzal all call North America home.

Diversity here doesn't just apply to animals and habitats. The descendants of the Native Americans who originally settled the land still strive to carry on their centuries-old cultures and traditions. But most North Americans are descendants of immigrants or slaves, making the continent rich with different languages, skin colors, food, and cultures.

People have long come to North America from other continents in search of opportunity. The Spanish sought gold in Mexico in the 1500s. French voyageurs explored the upper Great Lakes in the 1700s in birchbark canoes to make their fortune in the fur trade. Pioneers from across Europe staked out homesteads in the 1800s throughout the United States frontier. They're joined by millions of people today, drawn to industrialized cities like Mexico City and New York City (the largest cities in North America) to stake a claim of their own.

NORTH AMERICA

NORTH AMERICA FACTS

LAND AREA
9,449,000 square miles

NUMBER OF COUNTRIES 23

POPULATION
551,014,000

LARGEST METROPOLITAN AREA
Mexico City (20,446,000 people)

LARGEST LAKE
Lake Superior, stretching between the U.S. and Canada (31,700 square miles)

LARGEST COUNTRY
Canada (3,855,103 square miles)

DENSEST COUNTRY
Barbados (1,668 people per square mile)

LONGEST RIVER
Mississippi-Missouri, United States (3,710 miles)

HIGHEST POINT
Mount McKinley (Denali), Alaska, U.S. (20,320 feet)

HOW'S THE AIR UP THERE?

20 COOL THINGS

15 THE EASTERN SPOTTED **SKUNK** OF NORTH AMERICA DOES **A HANDSTAND** BEFORE IT SPRAYS.

16 THE STATUE OF LIBERTY'S FINGERNAILS ARE EACH SLIGHTLY **BIGGER** THAN THIS BOOK.

1 SNOWSHOE HARES ARE WHITE IN WINTER AND BROWN IN SUMMER.

2 LEGEND SAYS THAT AZTEC RULER **MOCTEZUMA** DRANK **50 CUPS** OF **CHOCOLATE** A DAY.

3 GUATEMALA'S CURRENCY IS NAMED THE **QUETZAL,** AFTER THE NATIONAL BIRD.

4 PANAMA CITY, PANAMA, IS THE ONLY CAPITAL WITH A TROPICAL **RAIN FOREST** IN THE CITY LIMITS.

5 ABOUT TWO-THIRDS OF ALL KNOWN **TORNADOES** OCCUR IN THE UNITED STATES.

17 PEOPLE IN THE UNITED STATES OWN ABOUT **86 MILLION CATS** AND **78 MILLION DOGS.**

LOOK OUT, DOGS—YOU'RE OUTNUMBERED!

6 A 95-MILE-LONG **UNDERGROUND RIVER** FLOWS BENEATH **MEXICO.**

7 THE **CORAL REEF SYSTEM** OFF BELIZE IS THE SECOND LARGEST IN THE WORLD.

18 IT TOOK **FIVE TO SIX MILLION** YEARS FOR THE **GRAND CANYON** TO FORM.

THAT'S ONE OLD CANYON.

14 MORE **DINOSAUR FOSSILS** HAVE BEEN FOUND IN **NORTH AMERICA** THAN ANYWHERE ELSE.

19 **ISLAND FOXES** ARE FOUND ONLY ON THE CHANNEL ISLANDS OFF THE COAST OF CALIFORNIA.

13 IN 2011, **CANADA** PRODUCED ENOUGH **MAPLE SYRUP** TO FILL **13 OLYMPIC-SIZE POOLS.**

20 **TEXAS** IS THE ONLY U.S. STATE THAT ALLOWS RESIDENTS **TO VOTE** FROM SPACE.

12 **BOBCATS** ARE THE MOST COMMON WILD CAT IN NORTH AMERICA.

8 **DEATH VALLEY,** CALIFORNIA, IS THE HOTTEST PLACE IN THE WORLD.

9 **TWENTY MILES** OF STREETS, SHOPS, RESTAURANTS, AND HOTELS LIE UNDERNEATH MONTREAL, CANADA.

10 DURING WAR, **ANCIENT MAYA** WARRIORS HURLED CONTAINERS FULL OF HORNETS AT ENEMIES.

11 OVER **80 PERCENT** OF CANADIANS LIVE WITHIN **100 MILES** OF THE U.S. BORDER.

DOLPHIN SMARTIES

LUCKY DOG!

THESE **INTELLIGENT SEA MAMMALS** SHOW OFF THEIR **SMARTS** WITH **QUICK-THINKING RESCUES** AND **CLEVER PROBLEM SOLVING.**

NEWBORN DOLPHINS HAVE A TINY PATCH OF HAIR ON THEIR CHINS.

DOLPHINS CAN **HEAR** SOUNDS UNDERWATER THAT ARE **15 MILES** AWAY.

CAN YOU HEAR US NOW?

DOLPHINS SLEEP WITH ONE EYE OPEN.

The three bottlenose dolphins frantically splashed and charged toward the seawall where Sam and Audrey D'Alessandro were walking. They'd often spotted bottlenose dolphins swimming in the canal behind their house in Marco Island, Florida. But they'd never seen

TURBO THE DOG HAS SOME DOLPHINS TO THANK!

them act like this before. "One of them got up on its tail," Sam says. "It headed to the corner and slapped its head and body down on a little patch of sand there. The dolphin did it three or four times."

The couple peered over the seawall. Shivering on the mound of sand, with water up to his waist, was a stranded dog! The Doberman pinscher was trapped eight feet below against the seawall, with no way to escape to land.

Turns out "Turbo" had been missing for 15 hours and apparently had tumbled into the canal. Audrey used a

ladder to rescue the exhausted pooch, who was too weak to bark or stand after his overnight ordeal. The dolphins swam away, their work there done.

"I'm convinced the dolphins knew that Turbo was in trouble," Sam says. "If the one dolphin hadn't been slapping its body on that sand, I never would have looked."

SMART SWIMMERS

Bottlenose dolphins are natural rescuers. They've been observed taking turns pushing hurt dolphins to the surface so they could breathe, and leading stranded whales out to sea. They've even protected swimmers from nearby sharks. Not many animals show this willingness to help others, and scientists believe it's one thing that sets dolphins apart from other creatures in the intelligence department. It shows an ability to understand a problem and then figure out how to solve it.

In fact, many consider these mammals to be second only to humans as far as smarts go. They can learn quickly and use these lessons to survive and thrive in their temperate and tropical habitats—including the waters around North America, where they're the most commonly seen species of dolphin. For instance, one wild bottlenose dolphin named Buster figured out how

to "debone" her cuttlefish meals by scraping the animal along the seafloor. Another got fed up when a pelican kept stealing its fish—and decided to use its dolphin beak to yank the pelican underwater and give the bird a "get out of here" scare.

TALKIN' THE TALK

Another way bottlenose dolphins show off their smarts is by "talking." Dolphins travel together by the dozens, and sometimes groups number more than a hundred. To communicate in such a large group, these savvy social creatures have a complex language of squawks, squeaks, clicks, and whistles. Calves develop their signature whistle as early as one month old and use it throughout their lives to greet other dolphins, just as you'd tell someone your first name.

Communicating also helps dolphins work together, whether it's herding schools of fish for a group feast or protecting their young from predators. Plus, they can tell each other when a boat is passing so the dolphins can catch a fun ride in the boat's wake. These guys are smart enough to know a perfect play break when they see it!

HOW DO YOU SAY "BIRD" IN DOLPHIN-SPEAK?

MORE ANIMALS OF NORTH AMERICA

A GREEN SEA TURTLE CAN HOLD ITS BREATH FOR FIVE HOURS. DURING THAT TIME ITS HEART BEATS ONLY ONCE EVERY NINE MINUTES.

GREEN SEA TURTLE

Newly hatched green sea turtles could teach a few things to the stars on the TV show *Survivor*—the hatchlings start out buried alive! After hatching from its buried egg, the one-ounce turtle must dig itself out of the sandy beach and frantically crawl to the nearby ocean. Hungry birds and crabs hover, ready for a tasty turtle treat. Bright lights confuse and lure the hatchlings away from the moonlit water. In all, only 1 in 1,000 turtles will reach adulthood. Then somehow, after ten years or more, females return to a beach near where they hatched—often up and down the Atlantic and Pacific coasts of North America—to lay 100 to 200 eggs.

HEY, GET OUT OF MY TREE!

MOUNTAIN LION

Mountain lions are like the spies of the animal kingdom. For starters, these stalkers have aliases! They're also known as pumas, cougars, or catamounts. And as with any good spy, you'll probably never see one. Shy and solitary, mountain lions are rarely seen by humans as they slink around the swamps and forests of Mexico and Central America, as well as those of the western United States and Canada. When they do appear, they're usually on the hunt, taking down game as big as elk with a powerful pounce and a fatal bite to the back of the neck.

A CLEVER MAN ONCE RESCUED THREE WET MOUNTAIN LION CUBS FROZEN TO RAILROAD TRACKS BY POURING WARM WATER OVER THEM TO MELT THE ICE.

BALD EAGLE

You don't need eagle eyes to see that this bird is not actually bald. Its name instead likely comes from a Middle English word, *balled*, which means "having a white spot." Fine white feathers first sprout on the bird's head and tail by age five. That makes them easy to spot as they soar overhead—and then dive-bomb at 100 miles an hour to grab a fish, fowl, or rodent with their sharp talons. Bald eagles have been the national emblem of the United States since 1782, but they live in Canada and Mexico too.

THE BIGGEST BALD EAGLE NESTS WEIGH UP TO 4,000 POUNDS.

THIS IS A WEIRD GAME OF FOLLOW THE LEADER.

EVEN THOUGH SHE WAS AT AN AGE WHEN SHE WOULD NORMALLY LIVE BY HERSELF, ONE FEMALE GRIZZLY BEAR STAYED WITH HER INJURED BROTHER FOR WEEKS TO CATCH SALMON FOR HIM.

GRIZZLY BEAR

The world is an all-you-can-eat buffet to grizzly bears. They'll stand in a river in the forests of northwestern Canada and Alaska to snap up salmon, or fill their bellies with berries, nuts, and leaves—lots of them. Occasionally they'll feast on deer and young moose. All that yummi-ness helps fatten up the grizzlies to survive up to seven months of hibernation. The anything-goes diet definitely works. Male grizzlies can tip the scales at 1,400 pounds!

MOOSE

Hide-and-seek is a tough game for a moose. True, their large hooves and stiltlike legs let them move easily and quietly through the forests of northern North America. And the surprisingly strong swimmers can disappear beneath the water's surface for more than 30 seconds. But a male's huge antlers—which can spread six feet across—make it tough to find a hiding spot. And their nonstop appetites often draw these 1,000-pound creatures out into the open and into urban areas. Plus, the males' loud bellows can be heard for miles, making it easy for females to find them.

THOSE ANTLERS WOULD MAKE A GOOD NEST HOLDER.

THE FLAP OF SKIN UNDER A MOOSE'S THROAT IS CALLED A BELL.

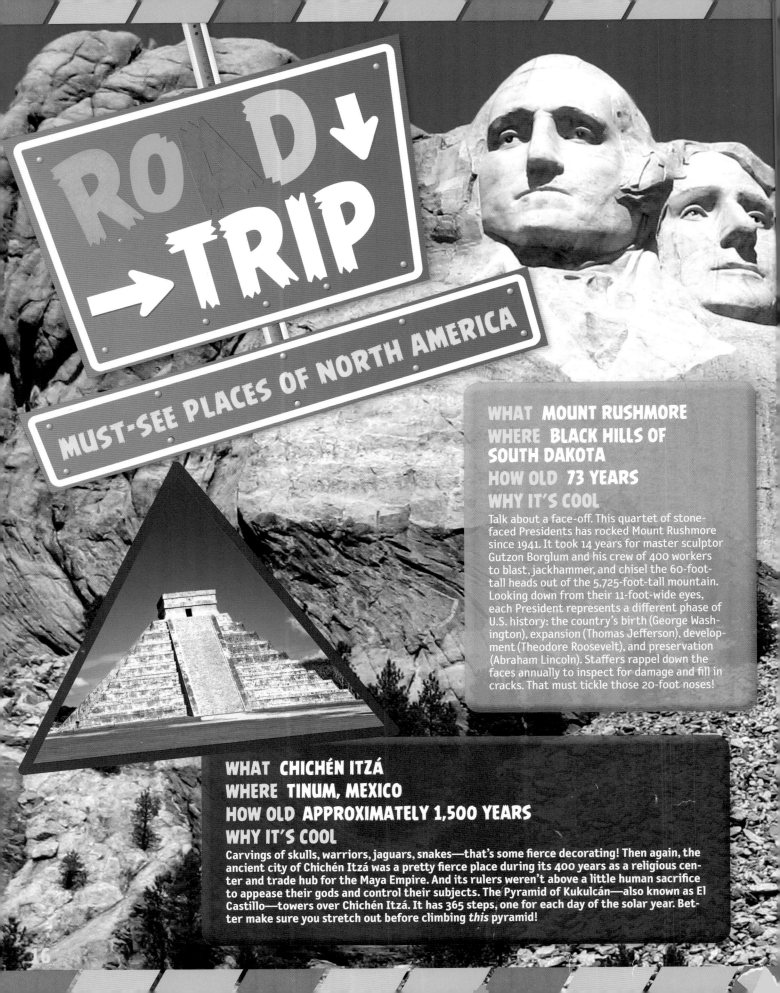

ROAD TRIP

MUST-SEE PLACES OF NORTH AMERICA

WHAT MOUNT RUSHMORE
WHERE BLACK HILLS OF SOUTH DAKOTA
HOW OLD 73 YEARS
WHY IT'S COOL

Talk about a face-off. This quartet of stone-faced Presidents has rocked Mount Rushmore since 1941. It took 14 years for master sculptor Gutzon Borglum and his crew of 400 workers to blast, jackhammer, and chisel the 60-foot-tall heads out of the 5,725-foot-tall mountain. Looking down from their 11-foot-wide eyes, each President represents a different phase of U.S. history: the country's birth (George Washington), expansion (Thomas Jefferson), development (Theodore Roosevelt), and preservation (Abraham Lincoln). Staffers rappel down the faces annually to inspect for damage and fill in cracks. That must tickle those 20-foot noses!

WHAT CHICHÉN ITZÁ
WHERE TINUM, MEXICO
HOW OLD APPROXIMATELY 1,500 YEARS
WHY IT'S COOL

Carvings of skulls, warriors, jaguars, snakes—that's some fierce decorating! Then again, the ancient city of Chichén Itzá was a pretty fierce place during its 400 years as a religious center and trade hub for the Maya Empire. And its rulers weren't above a little human sacrifice to appease their gods and control their subjects. The Pyramid of Kukulcán—also known as El Castillo—towers over Chichén Itzá. It has 365 steps, one for each day of the solar year. Better make sure you stretch out before climbing *this* pyramid!

WE'D LOOK SO GOOD NEXT TO THESE GUYS!

WHAT NIAGARA FALLS
WHERE BORDER BETWEEN THE CANADIAN PROVINCE OF ONTARIO AND NEW YORK STATE
HOW OLD APPROXIMATELY 12,000 YEARS
WHY IT'S COOL

Rain ponchos are a must for the 15 million people who visit Niagara Falls each year. Why? We're talking not one but *three* waterfalls—Horseshoe Falls, American Falls, and Bridal Veil Falls—thundering along the border between Canada and the United States. Those who take a boat ride on the *Maid of the Mist* right up to the base of the falls will get supersoaked. Other adventure seekers walk the Hurricane Deck, a wet and wild climb through the mist zone just feet from Bridal Veil Falls. A few crazy daredevils have taken the ultimate plunge: They rode over the approximately 185-foot Horseshoe Falls in barrels!

WHAT ENCHANTED HIGHWAY
WHERE REGENT, NORTH DAKOTA
HOW OLD 23 YEARS
WHY IT'S COOL

What do you get when a 45-foot-tall Tin Man meets a 51-foot-tall Teddy Roosevelt riding a horse? It's not some mixed-up version of *The Wizard of Oz*. They're among the seven enormous sculptures that appear along the 32-mile Enchanted Highway. Oil tanks, pipes, and barbed wire have been transformed into such gigantic works of art as a flock of ten airborne birds called "Geese in Flight" and a 40-foot-tall insect munching on grass entitled "Grasshopper's Delight."

DANCE MOVES

ONE NAVAJO TEEN KEEPS A TRADITION ALIVE WITH SOME FANCY FOOTWORK.

NAVAJO DANCERS (HERE AND BELOW) COMPETE DURING THE "GATHERING OF NATIONS," ONE OF THE LARGEST POWWOWS IN THE UNITED STATES.

A drum pounds out a steady beat. Tyler Yazzie jumps and spins around the dance floor like a tornado of color. Bells jingle on his legs. His brightly feathered headdress bounces to each boom. "I do a lot of moves: cartwheels, splits, lots of hopping," says Tyler, 13. "Sometimes I can really get into the song."

Tyler isn't dancing just for fun. The Navajo teenager from Battleford, Canada, is carrying on a Native American tradition—competing in the fancy feather dance, a popular event at powwows.

The fancy feather dance is relatively new—around 60 years old—compared to the Navajo people's long history. They settled in the American Southwest at least 600 years ago. Four sacred mountains mark the borders of the Navajo ancestral lands, which stretch through Arizona, Utah, and New Mexico.

The Navajo—who call themselves Diné, or "the people"—believe in maintaining harmony, or *hózhó*, among all living and nonliving things. They keep hózhó by doing good deeds and respecting the land. If an illness or another misfortune happens, a Navajo healer might perform a special ceremony to restore hózhó.

Today people of Navajo descent have settled across the continent and live just like anyone else in North America. But families keep Navajo heritage strong by passing on stories and skills such as jewelry making, weaving, and dancing. Tyler's dad taught his son his fancy feather moves. His father also keeps him calm before a competition. "I do get a little nervous, but once the drum starts, I'm good," he says. "I mean, I've been dancing ever since I could walk!"

MAKES ME WANT TO DANCE!

18

NICE FEATHERS.

TYLER YAZZIE WEARS AN OUTFIT HIS FATHER SEWED.

MOST **NAVAJO KIDS TODAY** LIVE JUST LIKE YOU DO. BUT HOW WOULD YOUR LIFE BE DIFFERENT IF YOU WERE A **NAVAJO KID IN THE 1850s?**

FOOD	wild game, squash, corn
HOUSE	a hogan, a circular-shaped, mud-covered earthen or wooden building
CHORES	babysit siblings, tend livestock, collect firewood, gather plants and herbs
CLOTHING	**Girls:** woolen dresses and sashes. **Boys:** woolen blankets, buckskin pants, and moccasins. Both wore silver jewelry.
FOR FUN	making string figures, competing in races—on foot or on a horse!

CELEBRATION OF LIGHT
VANCOUVER, CANADA

Vancouver celebrates with a bang during this *spark*-tacular three-night international fireworks competition. Teams set up their shots for the 25-minute musical fireworks extravaganzas. Some 400,000 spectators and judges take a bayfront seat to vote on which show was the biggest blast.

DAY OF THE DEAD (DIA DE LOS MUERTOS)
THROUGHOUT MEXICO

No bones about it: Day of the Dead is one of Mexico's liveliest celebrations. On November 1-2, families celebrate their deceased relatives by picnicking and sharing stories around their loved ones' graves. Women often dress up as skulls and skeletons, and kids snack on skull-shaped sweets.

CALAVERAS COUNTY FAIR AND JUMPING FROG JUBILEE
ANGELS CAMP, CALIFORNIA

On your mark, get set, *jump!* Every May, 50 frogs try to out-hop each other in the finals of this festival, hoping to beat Rosie the Ribiter's record of 21 feet 5¾ inches. A Mark Twain story called, um, "The Celebrated Jumping Frog of Calaveras County" inspired the first contest in 1893.

WELCOME TO SOUTH AMERICA

I HEAR THERE ARE LOTS OF BIRDS IN THE RAIN FOREST!

READY TO CHECK OUT SOUTH AMERICA!

THINK OF SOUTH AMERICA AS EARTH'S VERSION OF THE BIG DIPPER. THE HANDLE IS THE

towering Andes Mountains, stretching along this continent's western edge from Colombia down to southern Chile. Its highest reaches are home to some of the world's most complex radio telescopes, which peer into space searching for clues about how galaxies are formed.

The bowl is the Amazon Basin. The Amazon River flows through Peru and Brazil. It carries more water than the world's next ten biggest rivers combined. The Amazon rain forest, the world's largest, is home to everything from brightly colored poison dart frogs to secretive jaguars.

Some indigenous tribes, such as the Matis, still make their home deep in the Amazon rain forest. They strive to maintain their ancient traditions as the outside world gets closer and closer.

In fact, outsiders have dramatically shaped South America. Spanish and Portuguese invaders ruled most of the continent for almost 300 years. But the result is something exciting: The continent weaves together the traditions of the land's original inhabitants with European, African, and Asian heritages. People can rock out in masked parades, dance the tango, raft rain forest rapids—and eat tons of tasty food to fuel up for the next adventure.

SOUTH AMERICA FACTS

LAND AREA
6,880,000 square miles

NUMBER OF COUNTRIES 12

POPULATION
397,183,000

LARGEST METROPOLITAN AREA
São Paulo, Brazil
(19,924,000 people)

LARGEST LAKE
Maracaibo
(5,127 square miles)

LARGEST COUNTRY
Brazil
(3,287,612 square miles)

DENSEST COUNTRY
Ecuador (135 people per square mile)

LONGEST RIVER
Amazon (4,150 miles)

HIGHEST POINT
Cerro Aconcagua, Argentina
(22,831 feet)

WE CAN ALMOST SEE THE AMAZON RIVER FROM HERE!

SOUTH AMERICA

20 COOL THINGS

A DESERT PENGUIN? CRAZY!

1 A **PLANT** IN THE ANDES MOUNTAINS LIVES FOR ABOUT **80 YEARS.** IT FLOWERS ONCE, THEN DIES.

16 THE HUMBOLDT PENGUIN LIVES IN THE ROCKY DESERT COASTS OF CHILE AND PERU.

17 THE TALLEST **WATERFALL** IN THE WORLD, ANGEL FALLS IN VENEZUELA, IS TALLER THAN FIVE WASHINGTON MONUMENTS STACKED UP.

2 A **1,600-** YEAR-OLD TATTOOED **MUMMY** WAS DISCOVERED IN PERU.

18 SEVERAL **MILLION** SPECIES OF INSECTS LIVE IN THE **AMAZON RAIN FOREST.**

3 LEGEND HAS IT THAT A HOARD OF **INCA GOLD** IS BURIED DEEP INSIDE A MOUNTAIN CAVE IN ECUADOR.

19 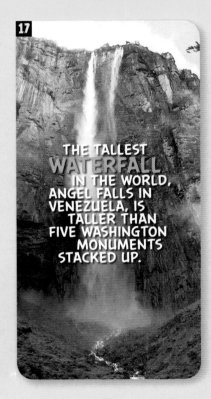 THE **MARINE IGUANA** LIVES ONLY ON THE **GALÁPAGOS ISLANDS,** IN ECUADOR.

4 AN EARTHQUAKE IN **CHILE** SHORTENED THE LENGTH OF AN EARTH DAY BY 1.26 MICROSECONDS.

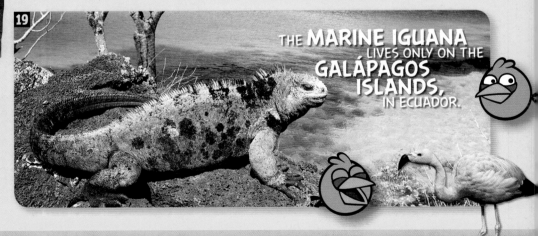

5 **MACAWS** OFTEN EAT CLAY.

6 IN **VENEZUELA,** YOU CAN PAY FOR THINGS WITH A **COIN** WORTH 12½ CÉNTIMOS.

7 **KINKAJOUS** CAN TWIST THEIR **HIND FEET** BACKWARD TO CLIMB TREES.

8 SOME **FLAMINGOS** LIVE IN THE CHILLY ANDES MOUNTAINS.

ABOUT SOUTH AMERICA

NICE FUR COAT.

20 OCELOTS EAT THE EQUIVALENT OF **FOUR TO FIVE** CANS OF CAT FOOD A DAY.

HOW WOULD WE LOOK IN PINK?

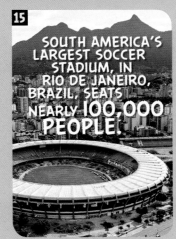

15 SOUTH AMERICA'S LARGEST SOCCER STADIUM, IN RIO DE JANEIRO, BRAZIL, SEATS NEARLY 100,000 PEOPLE.

14 SOME PEOPLE IN **PERU** WEAR **YELLOW UNDERWEAR** ON **NEW YEAR'S DAY** FOR GOOD LUCK.

13 THE BUS STATION IN LA PAZ, BOLIVIA, WAS DESIGNED BY **GUSTAVE EIFFEL,** THE SAME ARCHITECT WHO BUILT THE **STATUE OF LIBERTY** AND THE **EIFFEL TOWER.**

12 ROASTED ANTS ARE A POPULAR SNACK IN COLOMBIA.

9 ARGENTINA'S PERITO MORENO GLACIER STRETCHES MORE THAN **3 MILES LONG** AND NEARLY **200 FEET** ABOVE THE WATER.

10 THE AMAZON RAIN FOREST IS HOME TO GIANT RODENTS CALLED **CAPYBARAS** THAT ARE ABOUT AS TALL AS GERMAN SHEPHERDS.

11 NO COUNTRY IN SOUTH AMERICA HAS  EVER HOSTED THE OLYMPIC GAMES.

MONKEY TROUBLE

I LIKE THE SOUND OF TROUBLE.

GOLDEN LION TAMARINS HAVE A FIGHTING CHANCE IN THE FORESTS OF BRAZIL.

Eduardo the golden lion tamarin was on high alert. He and the eight other members of his family had just been relocated into the Poço das Antas Biological Reserve in southern Brazil, and so far this place was anything but home sweet home.

In their first week, the tiny maned monkeys had fought with bigger, faster capuchin monkeys, slept in a tangle of unprotected vines, and fled from another group of tamarins. And just as they were starting to feel safe in their new territory, the other tamarins were back—and they did not look happy.

But Team Eduardo had a secret—in the week since their confrontation, he and his family had learned how to fight back. So they arched their backs like Halloween cats. They sang out high, long calls and short "chuck" vocalizations to warn the other monkeys, "This is our turf—stay out!" Although tamarins rarely physically attack each other, Eduardo and crew chased the other tamarins back and forth across the boundary

THE TAIL OF A GOLDEN LION TAMARIN CAN BE NEARLY 15 INCHES—LONGER THAN THE REST OF ITS BODY.

and finally sent them packing.

"Getting to know the neighbors wasn't fun for these tamarins," says Jim Dietz, vice president of Save the Golden Lion Tamarin, which helped relocate the monkeys from an overcrowded forest to the reserve. "But their survival depended on being able to locate and successfully defend their own territory."

SURVIVORS

As one of the most endangered animals in the wild, the golden lion tamarin has been fighting not just for territory but for its very survival. They might be small—weighing less than two pounds and measuring about two feet long—but each tamarin group needs a territory of about a hundred acres. Because of deforestation for logging and farming, as well as urban expansion into the forests where they live, by the early 1970s, fewer than 200 were left in the wild.

But thanks to the work of scientists and conservationists, about 1,600 golden lion tamarins now live in protected areas such as the Poço das Antas Biological Reserve. Eduardo and his family were relocated there because the tiny patch of forest they had been living in didn't have enough food and other resources for them to survive.

WILD THINGS

The local conservationists have high hopes for the survival of Eduardo's family. The newcomers continue to roam the forest and have picked out a hollow tree where they can all safely sleep. During the day, they take to the tree canopy to search for food. They use their long, slender fingers to pluck fruit, nab a snail or lizard, snatch bird eggs, or probe under bark and in plants for insects. At least one adult always remains on the lookout. Their small size makes tamarins easy prey for hawks, jaguars, and boa constrictors.

Now the newcomers act just like their neighbors and they have been accepted by the larger tamarin community. "It's like Eduardo and his friends have earned the respect of the other tamarins," Dietz says. Looks like this neighborhood is growing into a full-on monkey town!

GOLDEN LION TAMARIN DADS OFTEN CARRY THEIR YOUNG ON THEIR BACKS IN BETWEEN FEEDINGS.

CAN I HITCH A RIDE TOO?

I WANT TO HANG OUT WITH THESE GUYS!

A GROUP OF TAMARINS IS CALLED A TROOP.

EDUARDO AND HIS TAMARIN FAMILY

MORE ANIMALS OF SOUTH AMERICA

THIS GUY'S SPOT-ON.

JAGUARS MAY SOMETIMES HANG OUT ON THE RIVER'S EDGE, TAPPING THEIR TAIL ON THE WATER TO ATTRACT HUNGRY FISH LIKE BAIT.

JAGUAR

Jaguar, leopard: Who can spot the difference? You can! A jaguar's circular pattern of dark spots, called a rosette, often has a dot in the center. Leopard spots don't. (Plus leopards live only in Asia and Africa.) These elusive hunters usually live in isolated pockets of rain forests, which are full of large prey like tapirs and peccaries. Scientists are now studying these pockets to see how the threatened cats use certain pathways to get from one pocket to another. That way, the conservationists can work with governments to protect those pathways from new highways, factories, or other obstacles.

GALÁPAGOS TORTOISE

Don't bother inviting a Galápagos tortoise to lunch. These slowpokes of the animal kingdom can go a whole year without eating or drinking. What do they do with all that free time? Sleep! They nap 16 hours a day. The tortoises were once so plentiful that the Spanish sailors who discovered the Galápagos Islands in 1535 chose the Spanish word for tortoise—*galápago*—as the name for their new territory. Unfortunately, those sailors—along with other explorers—hunted the creature to near extinction, and today only about 15,000 remain. Luckily, the Galápagos Islands, off the coast of Ecuador, are now a protected national park—so no need to *craawwll* away from hungry humans anymore.

A GALÁPAGOS TORTOISE NAMED HARRIET WAS THOUGHT TO HAVE LIVED TO BE 175 YEARS OLD.

TOCO TOUCAN

The fruit really flies when toco toucans are around. These playful, chatty birds like to woo potential mates with a good game of catch, tossing pieces of fruit back and forth with their colorful beaks. Those beaks—about the length of a banana—are handy tools in the rain forest canopies of such countries as Brazil, Argentina, and Paraguay. They use them to snatch eggs from trees, clean out their nests, nab fruit from branches, and even skin the occasional tasty lizard or frog. No wonder baby toucans leave the nest after six to eight weeks— they're ready to test out those amazing a-*bill*-ities!

> A TOUCAN BLENDS IN WELL WITH THE RAIN FOREST CANOPY, BUT THE BIRD IS SO NOISY THAT MOST ANIMALS KNOW EXACTLY WHERE IT IS!

THREE-TOED SLOTH

> A SLOTH WOULD TAKE A MONTH TO TRAVEL A SINGLE MILE.

Don't expect three-toed sloths to be getting a salon manicure anytime soon. Their long, strong nails are a must for survival. With curving claws, they clutch tightly to treetop branches in countries such as Brazil and Venezuela, nearly motionless, for up to eight days at a stretch. In fact, they move an average of only six to eight feet a minute, making them the slowest mammals on Earth. They're so slow that algae grows on their coat. No need to get them to the salon for a shampoo, though—the algae is actually good for them!

POISON DART FROG

Don't let their size fool you. Some of these two-inch-long amphibians have a poison powerful enough to kill ten grown men. Their bright colors are like warning labels, telling other animals in the rain forests of Brazil, Colombia, Ecuador, and Peru to stay away. Only the Emberá people dare to get close. They rub their blowgun darts on the frogs' backs to load the tips with toxins before a hunt. If they look closely, they just might spot a tadpole catching a froggyback ride on mom or dad. That's because some parents tote their recently hatched offspring—one at a time—to watery nurseries inside colorful flowering plants.

> SOME SCIENTISTS ARE TRYING TO TURN THE TOXIN FROM GOLDEN POISON DART FROGS INTO MEDICINE FOR HUMANS.

> WITH THOSE CLAWS, SLOTHS MUST BE AWESOME BACK SCRATCHERS.

ROAD TRIP

MUST-SEE PLACES OF SOUTH AMERICA

WELL, HELLO TO YOU TOO!

WHAT HAND OF THE DESERT
WHERE 45 MILES FROM ANTOFAGASTA, CHILE
HOW OLD 22 YEARS
WHY IT'S COOL

Now *that's* a high five! The 36-foot-tall Hand of the Desert emerges out of the Chilean desert landscape to wave to travelers along this desolate stretch of the Pan-American Highway. Created by Chilean artist Mario Irarrázabal, the iron and cement sculpture serves as a landmark for nearby Antofagasta, a city in Chile's remote copper-mining region. Unfortunately, vandals can't seem to keep their little hands off the ginormous one. That's why twice a year, volunteers spend 11 hours scrubbing the sculpture to keep it in top shape. Those guys are really lending a hand!

WHAT MOAI STATUES
WHERE EASTER ISLAND
HOW OLD 400 TO 600 YEARS
WHY THEY'RE COOL

It would sure help if these giant statues, called moai, could tell us how they became scattered across remote Easter Island, which is a part of Chile. But their enormous lips are sealed. Local legend says the moai walked to their current homes, powered by the spirits of ancestors. Scientists say it would've taken a ton of teamwork to move the nearly 300 statues into place without wheels or animals. First the statues—which average 13 feet high and 14 tons—were carved out of hardened volcanic ash. Islanders then might have tilted a statue onto its belly and rocked it side to side to move it as far as 11 miles away.

THAT IS ONE GIANT MONKEY.

WHAT NASCA LINES
WHERE NASCA, PERU
HOW OLD MORE THAN 2,000 YEARS

WHY THEY'RE COOL

From the air, the desert floor looks like a giant's chalkboard. There's a hummingbird that's as long as the Statue of Liberty (if the statue were lying down), a condor the length of nearly 11 school buses, and straight lines that stretch as far as 30 miles across the desert. The ancient Nasca people created some 1,200 of these glyphs, which today are called the Nasca lines. They likely staked out their patterns in teams, then turned over dark desert rocks to reveal the lighter sand underneath. Scientists think these amazing pictures were places of worship, where the Nasca made offerings and appealed to the gods for the one thing desert people need the most: water.

WHAT MACHU PICCHU
WHERE 50 MILES NORTHWEST OF CUSCO, PERU
HOW OLD ABOUT 550 YEARS

WHY IT'S COOL

Check out this supersecret hideout. Spanish invaders in the 1500s never discovered this remote Inca city nearly 8,000 feet up in the Andes Mountains. The Inca ruled much of western South America for nearly 300 years, and about 2,000 of them lived and farmed in this thriving community for a century. Their stone temples, houses, and terraces were built so well that it's said even a blade of grass can't fit between the stones. But then the city was abandoned, leaving it forgotten to the outside world until an American explorer stumbled upon it in 1911. Now 3,000 tourists a day visit the landmark to take in the same spectacular views the Inca enjoyed long ago.

TALK ABOUT FACES OF STONE!

HIDDEN PEOPLE

TAKE A PEEK AT THE MATIS— AN ISOLATED CULTURE THAT FEW PEOPLE HAVE EVER SEEN.

The good news: Dinner is here. The bad news: It's still alive and on the move, swinging about 90 feet up in the forest canopy. It's all in a day's meal, though, for the Matis people, an isolated indigenous tribe in the far western reaches of Brazil's Amazon rain forest. A Matis hunter raises a ten-foot-long blowpipe to his lips, aims carefully, and shoots a poison dart directly into the howler monkey. Bull's-eye!

For hundreds of years, the Matis people have lived untouched by the modern world, relying on the rain forest for their needs. But after their first contact with the outside world in the 1970s, the Matis tribe's chances for survival looked bleak. Like Europeans arriving in the New World, modern-day people accidentally introduced diseases that these jungle dwellers couldn't fight off. By 1983, only 87 Matis remained.

The Brazilian government now tightly controls access to the protected reserve where the Matis live. While the Matis have rebounded, their life today is different from when they moved through the jungles unknown to the outside world. Daily life still takes place around the *shobo*, a rectangular longhouse where the tribe eats and cooks

together and gathers for ceremonies and gossip. But tribe members are no longer nomadic; they've settled into just two villages with closer access to aid workers and medical help. Some younger Matis now attend school with other Brazilian kids, dress in Western clothing, and speak Portuguese in addition to the Matis language.

Elders, however, aren't letting the children forget their heritage. They're striving to revive cherished traditions, such as the tribe's well-known black-striped facial tattoos. And the Matis still rely on the jungle for their daily needs— and their skillful hunters to bring the feast home.

WONDER WHAT'S FOR DINNER?

PREPARING A MEAL

A HUNTER USES A BLOWPIPE.

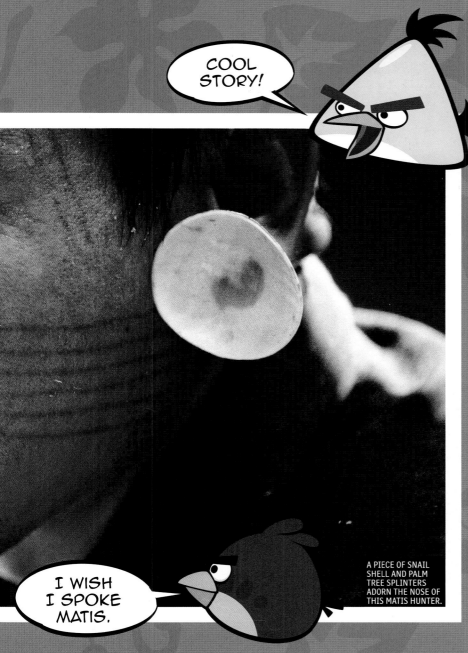

COOL STORY!

I WISH I SPOKE MATIS.

A PIECE OF SNAIL SHELL AND PALM TREE SPLINTERS ADORN THE NOSE OF THIS MATIS HUNTER.

HOW WOULD YOUR LIFE BE DIFFERENT... IF YOU WERE MATIS?

FOOD	monkey meat, eel, other fish, turtle eggs, green bananas
HOUSE	a *shobo,* a rectangular communal longhouse with a door that faces upriver
CHORES	carry water, gather wood
CLOTHING	Before outside contact, the Matis wore no clothes, only ornamental piercings and necklaces. Now some wear Western clothes.
FOR FUN	playing soccer, performing traditional dances

INTI RAYMI (FESTIVAL OF THE SUN)

OTAVALO, ECUADOR (AND OTHER CITIES ALONG THE ANDES MOUNTAINS)

Pack your swimsuit for this ancient Inca celebration, which honors the sun god in late June. Partiers break from daytime songs and dances that mark a good harvest in order to take a midnight dip in a nearby waterfall to cleanse their spirits. Now that's good clean fun!

TANGO FESTIVAL AND WORLD CUP

BUENOS AIRES, ARGENTINA

It takes two to tango, but 500,000 dance fans spin, slide, and kick their way through Argentina's capital every August to celebrate this famous dance where it was born. Free lessons teach the basic steps, while hundreds of pro dancers show how it's done—sometimes on the sidewalks!

CARNIVAL

RIO DE JANEIRO, BRAZIL

Crazy costumes and colorful masks welcome a new season every February or March. More than 5.3 million people party in the streets of Rio during this famous four-day festival. About 90,000 spectators fill a half-mile-long area to watch the wild Samba Parade, with fantastical floats and 3,000 to 5,000 singers, dancers, drummers, and marchers.

AMAZON ADVENTURE

The Angry Birds are ready to explore the Amazon rain forest. Each of these 12 small scenes is upside down or sideways. Find each small scene in the big picture.

ANSWERS ON PAGE 101

34

WELCOME TO EUROPE

BONJOUR, HOLA, GUTEN TAG, HELLO!

DINNERTIME JUST WOULDN'T BE THE SAME WITHOUT EUROPE.

TAKE ME TO THE KING!

Whether it's spaghetti and pizza from Italy, yummy cheeses from France and England, or delicious chocolates from Switzerland, this continent has everyone drooling. And those fairy tales your little sister or brother can't get enough of? Cinderella, Snow White, Hercules, and Hansel and Gretel are just a few of the once-upon-a-time characters that first sprang to life in Europe. After all, it's the land of real-life kings, princesses, and castles.

Over the centuries, this continent of nearly 50 countries has revolutionized industry, politics, art, and architecture. Ancient Greek and Roman civilizations left behind famous monuments such as the Parthenon and the Colosseum. The Greeks also developed the concept of democracy, while the Romans left behind the Latin language, which evolved into Italian, French, Spanish, and other common tongues spoken today by Europe's 740 million residents. The printing press, the "Mona Lisa," and even the Rubik's Cube come from Europe, which makes for some really cool bedtime stories that anyone would want to hear.

DUDE, WE JUST CROSSED AN OCEAN.

EUROPE FACTS

LAND AREA
3,841,000 square miles

NUMBER OF COUNTRIES
46

POPULATION
740,110,000

LARGEST METROPOLITAN AREA
Moscow, Russia
(11,621,000 people)

LARGEST LAKE
Caspian Sea
(143,200 square miles)

LARGEST COUNTRY
Russia
(6,592,850 square miles)

DENSEST COUNTRY
Monaco (45,000 people
per square mile)

LONGEST RIVER
Volga (2,290 miles)

HIGHEST POINT
El'brus, Russia (18,510 feet)

LAST ONE TO THE WINDMILL IS A ROTTEN EGG!

20 COOL THINGS

1 A MAN WALKED **ON HIS HANDS** FROM VIENNA, AUSTRIA, TO PARIS, FRANCE. THE TRIP TOOK **55 DAYS.**

2 A **DRAGON** STATUE BREATHES **FIRE** NEAR WAWEL ROYAL CASTLE IN KRAKÓW, POLAND.

3 AN ANNUAL FESTIVAL IN THE NETHERLANDS HONORS **REDHEADS.**

4 MOST **SWANS** IN ENGLAND BELONG TO THE **QUEEN.**

5 MORE **CHOCOLATE** IS CONSUMED IN SWITZERLAND THAN ANYWHERE ELSE IN THE WORLD— 23 POUNDS OF CHOCOLATE PER PERSON.

IT MAKES SENSE THAT I'M IN RED SQUARE.

14  *ROLLER-SKIING* IS A POPULAR SPORT IN NORWAY.

15 IN **MOSCOW'S** RED SQUARE IN RUSSIA (WHICH INCLUDES ST. BASIL'S CATHEDRAL), YOU CAN VIEW THE PRESERVED BODY OF FORMER RUSSIAN LEADER VLADIMIR LENIN THROUGH **A GLASS CASKET.**

6 A **CHILD'S FOOTPRINT** FOUND IN A **FRENCH CAVE** IS 25,000 YEARS OLD.

7 THE **RUBIK'S CUBE** WAS INVENTED IN HUNGARY.

ABOUT EUROPE

13 THE FIRST **JET PLANE** WAS FLOWN IN GERMANY.

16 A **REINDEER'S** NOSE HEATS UP AIR ON THE WAY TO ITS **LUNGS.**

12 IN PORTUGAL IT'S CONSIDERED RUDE TO WRITE IN **RED INK.**

11 THE MINUTE HAND OF LONDON'S **BIG BEN** CLOCK TRAVELS ABOUT 118 MILES A YEAR.

17 THE **MONA LISA** HAS NO EYEBROWS.

I CHALLENGE YOU TO A STARING CONTEST.

10 ABOUT **85 PERCENT** OF HOMES IN ICELAND ARE WARMED USING **UNDERGROUND** HEAT FROM GEOTHERMAL **HOT SPRINGS.**

19 ON SUNNY DAYS, THE **EIFFEL TOWER** IN PARIS, FRANCE, LEANS TOWARD THE SHADE.

20 CREATING **HUMAN TOWERS— SOME 35 FEET TALL—** IS A TRADITION IN SPAIN.

18 THE AVERAGE **HEDGEHOG** HAS 4,000 TO 7,000 **SPINES.**

8 THE LARGEST KNOWN ANT **SUPERCOLONY** STRETCHES NEARLY 4,000 MILES THROUGH PORTUGAL, SPAIN, FRANCE, AND ITALY.

9 THE **PARTHENON** WAS BUILT NEARLY 2,500 YEARS AGO TO HONOR THE **GREEK GODDESS ATHENA.**

SEALS OF APPROVAL

TWO MEDITERRANEAN MONK SEALS SHARE MOM DUTIES TO HELP A PUP SURVIVE.

MINTED IN 500 B.C., ONE OF THE WORLD'S FIRST COINS FEATURED THE HEAD OF A MONK SEAL.

SEALS ARE LUCKY—THEY DON'T NEED SNORKELS.

HOW ABOUT A GAME OF MARCO POLO?

Rosa Pires held her breath. For several weeks the biologist, along with nature rangers, had been monitoring remote Tabaqueiro Beach on Portugal's Desertas Islands, searching for a sign that some of the 40 critically endangered Mediterranean monk seals in the area had returned to the beach to give birth.

Suddenly one of the black rocks on the sand seemed to come to life. It was a newborn female monk seal, barely a day old. Pires was thrilled to see "Marver" snuggling next to her mother, named Female Y. But then the biologist got *really* excited. Marver was also cuddling up to an unrelated female named Riscagrande, who seemed to be sharing mom duties with Female Y.

"This meant that Marver had a real chance for survival," Pires says. "Two 'moms' watching over her meant that she had an excellent chance to grow up and have pups of her own."

RARE SEALS

The Mediterranean monk seal is the planet's most endangered pinniped, or fin-footed animal (which includes seals, sea lions, and walruses). Fewer than 600 remain, hiding out in caves and along the remote, rocky coasts of Greece, Turkey, and other scattered Mediterranean sites, as well as Mauritania.

Centuries ago in ancient Greece, fishermen and sailors considered it good luck to spot a Mediterranean monk seal.

But they later found the seals to be a nuisance. Each 550-pound adult monk seal can gobble up to 55 pounds of fish, lobsters, and jellyfish a day. That left less for the fishermen and caused conflict between seals and humans. The animals were also hunted for their fur, oil, and meat. To make things worse, overfishing, disease, and habitat loss drastically slashed their numbers.

BABYSITTERS' CLUB

Marver's story gives biologists hope for these endangered seals. With two moms to protect her, the newborn had a much better chance of surviving those perilous first few weeks. For instance, when Female Y swam out into the ocean to search for food, Riscagrande stayed with Marver on the beach, using her body to shield the newborn from waves that could crash ashore and drag the pup out to sea. Within two months, Marver was a strong enough swimmer to join her two moms in the deeper water.

Biologists like Pires have seen this "shared parenting" before. In fact, about nine years ago, Riscagrande came to this same beach as a young mother with her new pup. Two older female seals named Birisca and Desertinha were there too. The two experienced moms swung into service as nannies, and the three females switched off watching the pup while the others hunted for food. Perhaps all these years later, Riscagrande is simply returning the babysitting favors!

A MOTHER MONK SEAL CUDDLES WITH HER PUP.

NOW THAT THEY ARE BETTER PROTECTED, MONK SEALS CAN HANG OUT ON OPEN BEACHES INSTEAD OF IN CAVES.

MEDITERRANEAN MONK SEALS CAN HOLD THEIR BREATH FOR UP TO TEN MINUTES.

THE MERMAID MYTH MAY HAVE COME FROM SAILORS MISTAKING MONK SEALS FOR THOSE CREATURES.

MORE ANIMALS OF EUROPE

THIS PUFFIN DOESN'T LOOK SO "PUFFY" TO ME.

ATLANTIC PUFFIN

Atlantic puffins' brightly colored bills and silly appearance have earned these foot-high seabirds the nickname "clowns of the sea." That beak, however, is no joke—it's a serious fishing tool for catching and holding several small fish at a time as far down as 200 feet underwater off the coast of Iceland. Herring gulls try to steal the fish straight from the puffin's beak once it's airborne, but the laugh is usually on the gulls: Puffins can fly as fast as 55 miles an hour, like a car speeding along a highway.

SOME PEOPLE USED TO THINK PUFFINS—WHICH ARE GREAT SWIMMERS AND DIVERS—WERE PART FISH AND PART BIRD.

POLAR BEAR

What's black and white and warm all over? A polar bear! Its trademark white fur (which is actually clear but appears white because of sunlight) camouflages this powerful predator as it hunts in Europe's frozen Arctic landscape of northern Russia and Norway. But underneath, black skin helps the bear absorb the sun's warming rays. That's important during the long hours a polar bear spends on the sea ice, waiting for a tasty seal to pop up. Many scientists think climate change is causing the sea ice to melt faster, depleting the bears' hunting ground and forcing these fierce hunters to swim farther for food. To help protect polar bears, scientists are watching their movements across the changing landscape— that is, if they can spot them!

A POLAR BEAR'S PAW IS AS BIG AS A DINNER PLATE.

IS THERE ROOM FOR ONE MORE SNUGGLER?

IBERIAN LYNX

How can experts save the critically endangered Iberian lynx? Pull a rabbit out of a hat! Fewer than 300 of these big cats are left, in protected areas of southwestern Spain and possibly Portugal. Not only has the lynx's habitat been chopped down for highways and farms, but an epidemic depleted the lynx's primary food source, the European rabbit. Scientists are now successfully breeding captive lynx and releasing them into protected areas that are hopping with rabbits. Rabbit stew, anyone?

BARBARY MACAQUE

Unlike many other monkeys, the Barbary macaque does not have a tail. But boy, does this endangered monkey have a tale to tell. Living in Gibraltar's Upper Rock Nature Reserve, the creature is Europe's only free-ranging primate. In the 1940s only seven remained, so officials brought seven more from North Africa to jump-start the population. Today, an organization closely monitors Gibraltar's macaques and brings extra fruits and vegetables to supplement their natural diet of plants and flowers—and to discourage eating unhealthy (and illegal) handouts from tourists.

WANT TO HEAR OUR HOWLS?

GRAY WOLF

Gray wolf packs are a lot like your family. Older siblings babysit while Mom and Dad are busy. Parents keep the family safe and well fed. And family members "talk" to each other by howling, whining, and barking, and even with body language. But wolves—which in Europe live in pockets of forests from Greece to Sweden to Spain—aren't always thought of as tight-knit families. Many people see them as predators that destroy livestock. That's why scientists are helping farmers use electric fences and sheepdogs to better pro-tect their flocks, and teaching governments how to build safe crossing areas around highways. That's something to howl about.

WHAT COLOSSEUM
WHERE ROME, ITALY
HOW OLD 1,934 YEARS
WHY IT'S COOL

As you enter the ruins of this ancient stadium that at one time held 50,000 spectators, you can almost see the gladiator battles. Warriors and caged animals—lions, bison, bears, and elephants—hunkered in the corridors under the stadium while crowds poured in to take their seats. (Most women could sit only in the highest seats.) The stadium's first show might have been the most spectacular: Its opening in A.D. 80 was celebrated with a hundred days of games.

WHAT FLOATING WATER TAP
WHERE YPRES, BELGIUM
HOW OLD 11 YEARS
WHY IT'S COOL

If you overload on Belgian waffles and chocolates during your visit, you know where you can wash up afterward. This 12.5-foot-tall sculpture looks as if a running faucet is floating in the air, but it's just an illusion. A clear pipe inside the falling stream carries water from a pool on the ground to the faucet. The water loops around and is spewed back out over the pipe and into the pool so it looks like an unending gusher. Now, how do you turn it off?

TALK ABOUT ROCK 'N' ROLL.

WHAT STONEHENGE
WHERE SALISBURY PLAIN, ENGLAND
HOW OLD AROUND 4,500 YEARS
WHY IT'S COOL

This is one big history mystery. For hundreds of years scientists have been stumped with questions: How did ancient builders move the stones—weighing between 8,000 and 100,000 pounds? What was the purpose of this massive stone monument? As a way to observe the sun and stars? As a place of healing? Scientists know one thing for sure: Stonehenge became a cemetery, with some 200 burials on the grounds. But who's buried beneath the stones? As long as these mysteries remain, Stonehenge lore will rock on for years to come.

REINDEER 101

SAMI KIDS TAKE CLASSES IN READING, WRITING, AND—YEP!—REINDEER HERDING AT THIS SPECIAL SCHOOL.

Think it's a chore to walk your dog outside when it's cold? Try watching your family's reindeer herd near the Arctic Circle! Johan Ante Buljo has been learning reindeer herding from his relatives since he was about ten, but for high school, he enrolled in the Sami High School and Reindeer Management School in Kautokeino, Norway. There he joined other teenagers to study reindeer herding, a Sami cultural tradition.

For generations, Johan's family and other people of the Sami culture—who live in Norway, Sweden, Finland, and a small corner of Russia—have lived as roaming reindeer herders. Relying on this hardy animal for food, clothing, and transportation, the Sami move the herd from its winter home on the plains to coastal areas in the spring, where females give birth. The Sami are sort of like American cowboys, except they sleep in circular tents called *lávvu* instead of under the stars and use snowmobiles instead of horses to round up reindeer.

Sami High School is just like any high school, where students take classes in literature, math, and science. But because many kids will eventually take

over their families' herd, they also study...reindeer. They sew coats, hats, and gloves from reindeer hides, and carve knives out of antlers and bone. They learn about land management and master snowmobile maintenance.

"To work with reindeer, you need to know many different things: repairing vehicles, managing the herd, and how to be patient," Johan says.

During school breaks, students rejoin their on-the-move families to test their new skills. Johan particularly enjoys the summertime "marking," in which calf ears are notched with a family's signature mark.

"It's an old tradition, and you inherit a design from your family," he says. "My main design comes from my great-grandfather, but with a few alterations to make it my own."

THOSE ARE SOME WEIRD-LOOKING HORSES.

REINDEER SLEDDING IS A POPULAR ACTIVITY AMONG MANY SAMI PEOPLE.

MY TURN, MY TURN!

A SAMI HIGH SCHOOL STUDENT HARVESTS SEDGE GRASS TO USE AS STUFFING FOR REINDEER-SKIN BOOTS.

A SAMI GIRL LEADS REINDEER AT THE START OF THE SPRING MIGRATION.

HOW WOULD YOUR LIFE BE DIFFERENT...
IF YOU WERE TRADITIONAL SAMI?

FOOD	reindeer meat, fish, potatoes, wild celery, berries, mushrooms
HOUSE	a *lávvu*, a circular tent similar to a tepee
CHORES	cook meals, wash dishes, keep track of supplies, watch reindeer
CLOTHING	*gakti*, a brightly colored high-collared embroidered tunic; reindeer-leather coats and hats
FOR FUN	reindeer racing, singing traditional songs called *joik*

START THE PARTY, EUROPE STYLE!

FLOWER PARADE
TOWNS AROUND BELGIUM AND THE NETHERLANDS
Don't try to tiptoe through these tulips—they might run you over! Millions of tulips, dahlias, and other blooms transform into giant floats such as bees, elephants, and pirate ships for the traditional flower parades held in spring and fall.

KALTENBERG KNIGHTS TOURNAMENT
GELTENDORF, GERMANY
Have fun storming the castle—the 13th-century Kaltenberg Castle, that is—to watch more than a thousand performers bring the Middle Ages to life. During this July festival, the arena rocks, um, "knight after knight" with daring sword fights, royal rescues, and a hard-charging jousting competition. *En garde!*

LA TOMATINA FESTIVAL
BUÑOL, SPAIN
You say to-*may*-to, I say to-*mah*-to. But in Buñol, they say *splat!* as 50 tons of tomatoes go flying in the town's annual food fight in August. What started in the 1940s as a local affair now attracts 40,000 people who are definitely seeing red by the day's messy end.

FREE FALL

AWK!

A LITTLE TO THE LEFT, GUYS.

The Angry Birds are flying over Italy's Tower of Pisa. Someone has forgotten a guidebook at the top of the tower. Using the series of clues, figure out which person the guidebook belongs to.

ANSWER ON PAGE 102

The person whom the guidebook belongs to...

- is wearing glasses.
- is not wearing a hat.
- has brown hair.
- is wearing a watch.
- is wearing a short-sleeved shirt.
- is wearing red shoes.

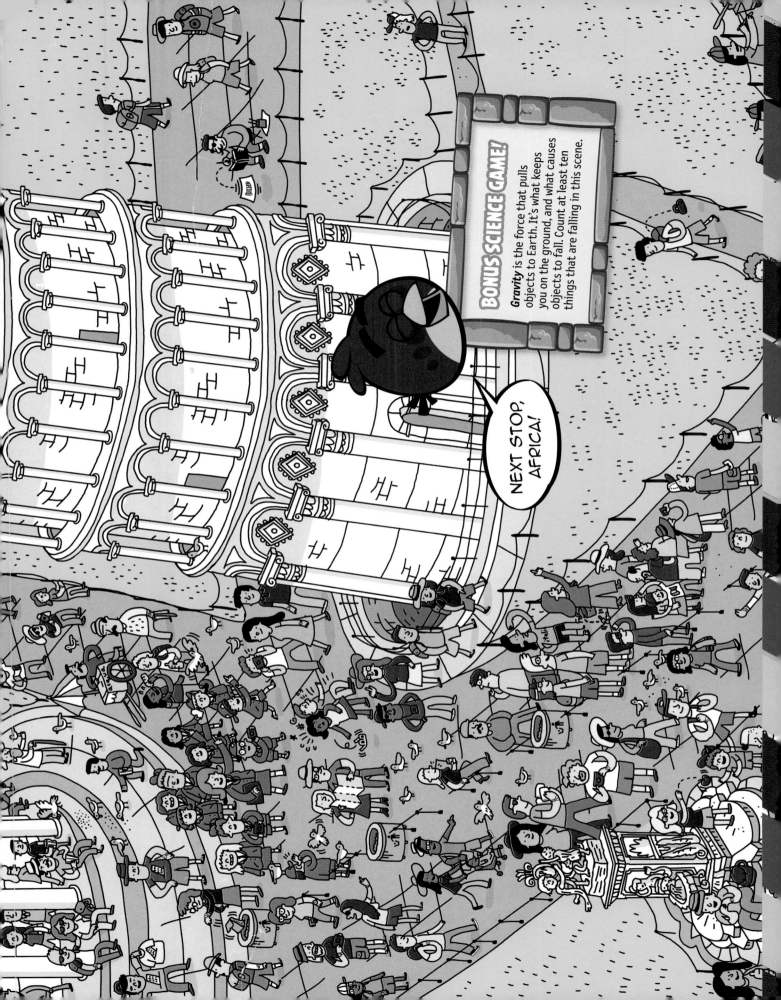

WELCOME TO AFRICA

WOO-HOO, AFRICA!

ROARING LIONS, THUNDERING ELEPHANTS, LIGHTNING-FAST CHEETAHS. FROM THE CAMELS

plodding across the blazing-hot sands of the Sahara to the wildebeests migrating through the Great Rift Valley, wildlife is often the first thing people picture when they think about Africa.

But Africa isn't just all animals, all the time. Today more than a billion people live on this enormous continent. They represent an amazing range of cultures, from the traditional tribal life of the Maasai in Kenya and Tanzania to the modern hustle and bustle in booming cities such as Lagos, Nigeria. Some 2,100 languages—from Arabic to French to Zulu—are spoken in Africa, second only to Asia.

Many countries in Africa remain poor, but the continent's economy is growing faster than any other. And more kids are going to school, and for longer. Plus, Africans are optimistic about their future. That's plenty of good news to roar about!

CAN'T WAIT TO SEE SOME LIONS AND ELEPHANTS!

I HEAR THEY HAVE PINK BIRDS IN AFRICA!

AFRICA FACTS

LAND AREA
11,608,000 square miles (second only to Asia)

NUMBER OF COUNTRIES
54 (more than any other continent)

POPULATION
1.07 billion

NUMBER OF LANGUAGES
Some 2,100

LARGEST METROPOLITAN AREA
Lagos, Nigeria (estimated 11 million people)

LARGEST LAKE
Victoria
(26,800 square miles)

LARGEST COUNTRY
Algeria
(919,595 square miles)

DENSEST COUNTRY
Mauritius (1,639 people per square mile)

LONGEST RIVER
Nile (4,160 miles)

HIGHEST POINT
Kilimanjaro, Tanzania
(19,340 feet)

51

20 COOL THINGS

1 A **LIZARD** IN MADAGASCAR HAS A **THIRD EYE** ON TOP OF ITS HEAD.

2 A **METEOR CRATER** IN SOUTH AFRICA IS WIDER THAN **IRELAND.**

3 A MALE AFRICAN **CICADA** CAN MAKE A SOUND **AS LOUD AS** A POWER MOWER.

4 AN **OSTRICH'S EYE** IS LARGER THAN ITS BRAIN.

5 ZIMBABWE ISSUED A **ONE-HUNDRED-TRILLION-DOLLAR** BANKNOTE THAT WAS NEVER WORTH **MORE THAN $40.**

14 A **CHEETAH** CAN CHANGE DIRECTION IN **MIDAIR** WHEN **CHASING PREY.**

YOU SHOULD SEE SOME OF MY MIDAIR TRICKS!

15 SOME SCENES IN THE **STAR WARS MOVIES** WERE FILMED IN TUNISIA.

16 THE **SAHARA DESERT** IS ABOUT THE SAME SIZE AS THE **UNITED STATES.**

6 AFRICA'S ARABIAN **CAMELS** HAVE ONE HUMP; **BACTRIAN CAMELS** IN ASIA HAVE TWO.

7 A **CANNON** CALLED THE **NOON GUN** IS FIRED EVERY DAY AT, UH, **NOON** IN CAPE TOWN, SOUTH AFRICA.

ABOUT AFRICA

13 AFRICAN **PENGUINS** FACE LAND PREDATORS SUCH AS LEOPARDS, SNAKES, AND MONGOOSES.

17 THE **NILE RIVER** IS LONGER THAN THE DISTANCE FROM WASHINGTON, D.C., TO LOS ANGELES, CALIFORNIA.

18 **LEMURS** FROM MADAGASCAR CAN WEIGH AS LITTLE AS **FIVE QUARTERS** OR AS MUCH AS A **CAR TIRE**.

12 SOUTH AFRICA'S GIANT **BULLFROG** SOMETIMES **ATTACKS LIONS**.

11 JUST TWO DROPS OF VENOM FROM AFRICA'S **BLACK MAMBA**, ONE OF THE WORLD'S DEADLIEST SNAKES, CAN KILL A HUMAN.

10 **KING TUT'S BURIAL MASK** WAS MADE WITH MORE THAN **20 POUNDS** OF SOLID GOLD.

WONDER IF HIS YODEL ECHOES OFF MOUNTAINS?

20 THRILL-SEEKING TOURISTS **SANDBOARD** DOWN GIANT DUNES ON MANY OF AFRICA'S BEACHES AND DESERTS.

9 **RHINO HORNS** ARE MADE OF THE SAME SUBSTANCE AS HUMAN **FINGERNAILS**.

19 THE **BASENJI,** A DOMESTICATED **DOG** FROM AFRICA, **YODELS** INSTEAD OF BARKS.

8 MORE THAN HALF OF THE **3.2 MILLION PEOPLE** LIVING IN DAR ES SALAAM, THE CAPITAL OF TANZANIA, ARE **KIDS OR TEENS**.

LION PRIDE

PRIDE

FAMILY LIFE FOR THESE BIG CATS MEANS FOOD, PROTECTION—AND LOTS OF FRIENDS TO HANG WITH.

Sharp cries fill the air. A lion cub clings to a cliff wall in Kenya's Masai Mara National Reserve. In the river below, hungry crocodiles wait for just one slip—and an easy meal.

Up above, the cub's mother and four other members of her pride claw at the ledge. They attempt to climb down to rescue the stranded cub, but they're stopped by the steep slope. The mother lion can't wait and springs into action.

Using her strong paws, she carefully edges down the nearly vertical slope toward her exhausted cub. Just as the little lion seems about to slip, his heroic mom swoops under him and scoops him up in her mouth. She carries him back up the cliff, out of danger. The supportive pride looks on in relief as the mother comforts her cub with gentle licks on his head.

ALL IN THE FAMILY

Members of a lion pride have each other's back. While other big cats prefer to live alone, lions work together to survive in the grasslands and deserts of Africa. Prides can number anywhere from 3 to 40 lions, with a few males in the mix as fathers and protectors.

All the lionesses in a pride are related: Moms, aunts, sisters, and grandmothers share their territory and raise their

cubs as a family. For the cubs, it's like nonstop recess: All those brothers, sisters, and cousins make great playmates.

Just like house cats, cubs love to pounce: on twigs, on their mom's twitching tail, and on each other. But they're not just playing. Their "games" are teaching them how to be predators. After three months, the cubs start tagging along on the real hunts and learn by watching Mom in action.

CHOW TIME

Lions are kings—and queens—of the food chain. Still, the pride must work together to make sure there's enough food for everyone. The lionesses usually set out at dusk or dawn in search of a meal, such as a tasty wildebeest or antelope. The smaller females chase the prey toward the pride, where the larger lionesses pounce. By working together, there's less risk of a lion getting injured.

Sometimes when there's not enough food, lions prey on domesticated

WATCH OUT. YOU DON'T WANT HIM COVERED IN DROOL!

animals such as cows and other livestock. Farmers try to protect their herds with *bomas*, or pens enclosed by big branches. But they usually aren't strong enough to keep out the big cats. Conservationists are now working with farmers to help them build strong wire bomas. That keeps the livestock safe from lions— and the lions safe from angry farmers.

By the time the cubs turn two, there are no more free meals. Females graduate to the family hunting pride. As for their brothers, it's time to hit the road. They'll wander in groups or by themselves, in search of another pride to call their own.

MORE ANIMALS OF AFRICA

KEEP IT DOWN, WILL YA?

ELEPHANT

African elephants may look like they're all ears. But these six-ton creatures also use some fancy footwork to listen to each other. When elephants make low-frequency rumbles or stomp their feet, the vibrations travel through the ground. Other elephants pick up these messages from as far as ten miles away through thick, spongy pads on their feet. Although elephants in southern and eastern Africa are not as threatened, pachyderms in western and central Africa are in danger. One reason is because of conflicts with humans, such as elephants trampling crops or property. Thankfully, conservationists are teaching people how to live peacefully with elephants. That will give the world's largest land animal something to yell about—especially since their calls can be heard over a hundred-square-mile area!

A FAMILY OF ELEPHANTS BUILT A DIRT RAMP WITH THEIR TUSKS SO A BABY COULD CLIMB OUT OF A HOLE IT HAD FALLEN INTO.

HIPPOPOTAMUS

With their short, stocky legs and ginormous bodies, hippos may seem a little clunky on land. But the four-ton creatures are much more graceful in slow-moving rivers and lakes. Hippos have no true sweat glands, so they cool off by staying submerged with only their eyes, ears, and nostrils breaking the water's surface. When they're ready for a full-body dip, they can stay under for up to five minutes. Their lungs must be huge!

A YOUNG ORPHANED HIPPO NAMED OWEN WAS "ADOPTED" BY A TORTOISE.

I WISH I HAD MY BATHING SUIT.

LESSER FLAMINGO

You are what you eat—especially if you're a lesser flamingo. Their pink and red feathers come from the colors of the algae and small crustaceans they eat in the lagoons and shallow lakes where they live. And when they're not eating, they're "dancing," hoping to wow a mate. Tens of thousands of flamingos will march together, then suddenly change direction. They'll turn their heads, twist their necks, even kick out a leg and a wing. It's like a flamingo hokey pokey.

A FLAMINGO NAMED ANDY ONCE TRIED TO HATCH A ROCK BECAUSE HE THOUGHT IT WAS AN EGG.

GIRAFFE

What if you spent most of your day eating and less than half an hour sleeping? Welcome to the life of a giraffe! As the tallest land mammal, giraffes need lots of food to fuel bodies that can grow up to 18 feet tall. In fact, one giraffe can eat up to 75 pounds in a day. To reach its favorite food—acacia tree leaves—a giraffe stretches its 6-foot-long neck and slides its 21-inch tongue around thorns to snag a few leaves at a time. No wonder eating takes all day.

HUNGRY MUCH?

AT A HOTEL IN KENYA, GIRAFFES STICK THEIR HEADS THROUGH OPEN WINDOWS TO EAT OFF GUESTS' TABLES.

NEED A HAIRCUT?

MOUNTAIN GORILLA

Male mountain gorillas have been known to pound their chest, roar, and throw branches to frighten younger rivals challenging them to be top ape. But despite their powerful King Kong image, these gentle creatures are endangered. Much of the gorillas' natural habitat has been destroyed as people clear the mountainous forests for farming and lumber. But thanks to efforts protecting the animal and its habitat, the wild population of mountain gorillas has gone from about 620 in 1989 to some 880 today. That's good news for the gorillas—and *fun* news for babies, who like to ride piggyback on their moms!

GORILLAS HAVE BEEN OBSERVED DISMANTLING TRAPS SET BY POACHERS.

ROAD ↓ →TRIP

MUST-SEE PLACES OF AFRICA

WHAT BIG PINEAPPLE
WHERE BATHURST, SOUTH AFRICA
HOW OLD 23 YEARS
WHY IT'S COOL

This three-story bright-yellow pineapple looks good enough to eat. But you'll have to settle for the pineapple jam in the gift shop, because the 55-foot-tall landmark is made of fiberglass, steel, and concrete. Stand on the Big Pineapple's third-floor observation deck and you'll see rolling pine-apple fields, which makes sense—the huge fruit celebrates the region's booming pineapple industry. Bathurst is in an area known as the Sunshine Coast. All those rays have enabled pineapple farms to flourish here for more than a hundred years. Just don't mistake this structure for Australia's Big Pineapple—that one is two feet shorter!

HEY, I LOOK KIND OF LIKE A LITTLE PINEAPPLE!

WHOA! THERE WERE MUMMIES IN THESE THINGS!

WHAT **PYRAMIDS AT GIZA**
WHERE **NEAR CAIRO, EGYPT**
HOW OLD **CONSTRUCTION STARTED ABOUT 4,600 YEARS AGO**
WHY THEY'RE COOL

When you're a great pharaoh, why think small? The Pyramids at Giza are the final resting place for three Egyptian rulers and their families. Pharaoh Khufu's Great Pyramid is the oldest and tallest, topping out at 481 feet. Hieroglyphs—a form of ancient writing involving symbols—spelled out for scientists exactly who was buried there. Of course, Khufu didn't actually build his pyramid himself. Archaeologists believe that some 36,000 workers labored over three decades hauling the millions of stone blocks into place. Some of the blocks weighed as much as six white rhinos!

FORGET HIKING THIS MOUNTAIN, I'M FLYING TO THE TOP!

CHECK OUT THE FALLS' LOCAL NAME: MOSI-OA-TUNYA.

WHAT **VICTORIA FALLS**
WHERE **BORDER OF ZAMBIA AND ZIMBABWE**
HOW OLD **OVER 2 MILLION YEARS**
WHY IT'S COOL

Pack a raincoat if you're visiting Victoria Falls—you'll probably get drenched! In fact, so much water is churned up by the roaring Zambezi River crashing over the fall's ledge that the mist can be seen as far away as 12 miles. The 354-foot waterfall was named for England's Queen Victoria in 1855 by the first European to see the falls, who spotted it from a small canoe. Nowadays tourists take a short hike to reach the mile-wide waterfall. On second thought, pack a raincoat *and* an umbrella!

WHAT **MOUNT KILIMANJARO**
WHERE **TANZANIA**
HOW OLD **PROBABLY 750,000 YEARS**
WHY IT'S COOL

Here's some good news for the thousands of hikers who climb Kilimanjaro each year. Although scientists think the 19,340-foot mountain was formed by volcanic activity, only one of its three volcanic peaks occasionally gives off gas and steam. On the way to the snowcapped peak (yep, snow in Africa!) they might see black-and-white colobus monkeys and blue-and-green malachite sunbirds. Plus they'll have reached "the roof of Africa." Why? Kilimanjaro is the highest point on the continent.

THE NAME GAME

HOW MAASAI KIDS GET THEIR "REAL" NAME YEARS AFTER THEY'RE BORN

WOO-HOO! Spring break! But 11-year-old Silvia Soit isn't hanging out at the beach or zipping down ski slopes. Instead, she's traveling home from the Mara Hills Academy boarding school to her village of Olesere, Kenya. The occasion? She'll be joining the celebration of a Maasai naming ceremony.

For about a thousand years, the Maasai people have roamed the grasslands of East Africa, leading their cattle across grassy plains from one watering hole to the next. Over the past century, however, changes in things such as transportation and technology have affected the Maasai's ways in Kenya and Tanzania. But even though some Maasai have left their villages for city life, and many children like Silvia attend modern schools with email and cell phones, Maasai are keeping their traditions alive.

The naming ceremony is an important moment in a Maasai kid's life. Around the age of two or three, Maasai children leave behind a temporary name given to them at birth and receive the name they'll have for life. Two people close to

the family help pick a good name. Originality is a must—no repeats of other family members' names are allowed!

The child sits together with Mom— and then the grandmother completely shaves both the mom's and kid's heads! The child is then introduced to the community for the first time by his or her new name. "It's like a new beginning in the life of the child," Silvia says.

Villagers look forward to naming ceremonies as kids in the United States might look forward to birthday parties. Silvia wears bracelets and three *shukas*, colorful sheets of cloth that wrap over her shoulders and around her body. She and her "age mates"—the group of kids in her village about her age—dance and sing their favorite chants, or *nambas*. It's a wild spring break!

DIFFERENT-COLORED GARMENTS AND BEADWORK OFTEN DISTINGUISH ONE GROUP OF MAASAI FROM ANOTHER.

MAASAI GIRLS IN TRADITIONAL DRESS

LOOKS LIKE THEY'RE HAVING A BLAST!

A MAASAI WOMAN IN TANZANIA BALANCES A BUCKET ON HER HEAD TO CARRY WATER.

MAASAI WARRIORS TRY TO OUTJUMP EACH OTHER IN A TRADITIONAL DANCE.

YEAH, CAN WE JOIN THE FUN?

HERMANUS WHALE FESTIVAL
HERMANUS, SOUTH AFRICA
Southern right whales make a big splash at this festival. The celebration in September marks the return of these mammals along the South African coast, where they mate, calve, and nurse their young. Lots of fun activities happen onshore, but all eyes are on the water to watch these 60-ton giants.

DOGON MASK FESTIVAL
MALI
Nope, it's not Halloween! The Dogon people of Mali wear these elaborate masks in different festivals during the spring to help spirits of deceased tribe members into the afterlife. Dancers wear the masks, which represent monkeys, rabbits, antelope, and other creatures.

INTERNATIONAL FESTIVAL OF THE SAHARA
DOUZ, TUNISIA
If this were a TV show, it'd be called *Sahara's Got Talent*. For more than a century, people from across the northern Sahara have gathered in December to celebrate the Berber and Bedouin cultures. Traditional dancing, camel and horse races, and storytelling bring on the fun.

HOW WOULD YOUR LIFE BE DIFFERENT...
IF YOU WERE TRADITIONAL MAASAI?

FOOD	mutton and goat meat, fresh or fermented milk
HOUSE	one-room hut made of cow dung, mud, and straw
CHORES	**Girls:** cook and carry firewood. **Boys:** tend livestock
CLOTHING	*shukas*, colorful sheets of cloth that wrap over the shoulders and around the body; colorful beaded jewelry
FOR FUN	practicing throwing arrows and spears, playing hide-and-seek

WELCOME TO ASIA

I HEAR RED IS A LUCKY COLOR.

TALK ABOUT AN EXTREME CONTINENT. DESCRIBING ASIA MEANS USING THE WORD "MOST" OR WORDS ENDING

in "-est" a lot. The largest of all seven continents sprawls across almost half the globe, with more than 40 countries stretching from western Turkey to the eastern tip of Russia. In between lie both the highest (Mount Everest) and lowest (the Dead Sea) places on Earth.

Asia's landmass is huge, and the continent is packed with people! It has the biggest population of any continent—in fact, Asia's four billion people (that's three out of every five people on the planet!) is more than all the other continents' populations combined. No wonder

Asia boasts the most million-plus cities, from Riyadh, Saudi Arabia, to Tokyo, Japan. But these bustling cities are hardly new to Asia. The first known civilization arose in Sumer, in what is now Iraq.

The influential people and cultures that have emerged in places such as India and China have given civilization some truly amazing landmarks, such as the Taj Mahal and the Great Wall of China. And the world's tallest building—the Burj Khalifa in Dubai, United Arab Emirates—stands in Asia, as do 13 of the Earth's 15 tallest skyscrapers. It looks like in Asia, even the buildings are extreme!

20 COOL THINGS

TWO KINDS OF PANDAS? WHO KNEW?

1 SOME COBRAS CAN SPIT VENOM OVER 6 FEET.

2 OFTEN FOUND IN THE INDIAN OCEAN, GIANT WAVES CALLED TSUNAMIS CAN CAUSE COASTAL SEA LEVELS TO RISE 30 FEET OR MORE.

16 A RED PANDA'S TAIL CAN BE 20 INCHES LONG—ALMOST THE LENGTH OF ITS BODY.

QUITE A "TAIL" TO TELL.

3 THE BIGGEST INHABITED PALACE ON EARTH, IN THE SOUTHEAST ASIAN COUNTRY OF BRUNEI, HAS 1,788 ROOMS.

17 THE 50 TALLEST MOUNTAINS IN THE WORLD ARE ALL IN ASIA.

4 A TRAFFIC JAM IN CHINA LASTED FOR MORE THAN A WEEK.

5 THE NAME OF THE PHILIPPINES' PRESIDENT ARROYO WAS MISSPELLED AS ARROVO ON THE HUNDRED-PESO NOTE IN 2005.

6 SCIENTISTS WERE SHOCKED TO FIND THE COELACANTH (SEE-LAH-KANTH), WHICH THEY THOUGHT WAS EXTINCT, LIVING IN THE INDIAN OCEAN.

ABOUT ASIA

FORTUNE COOKIES ORIGINATED IN JAPAN, NOT CHINA. **15**

18 YOU CAN TELL AN ASIAN ELEPHANT FROM AN AFRICAN ELEPHANT BY ITS **SMALLER, ROUNDER EARS.**

14 **FRIED TARANTULAS** ARE CONSIDERED A DELICACY IN CAMBODIA.

13 BUILDERS OF JAPAN'S **NIJO CASTLE** CREATED **SQUEAKY FLOORS** TO PREVENT STEALTHY INTRUDERS.

12 IN TAIWAN, GARBAGE TRUCKS **BLAST MUSIC** TO REMIND PEOPLE TO BRING OUT THE TRASH.

HE MUST GET TONGUE-TIED!

19 A MALAYAN SUN BEAR'S **TONGUE** CAN BE A **FOOT LONG.**

11 A HOTEL IN CHINA IS ACTUALLY A **TREE HOUSE.**

20 THE **HIMALAYA MOUNTAINS** GROW A HALF INCH EACH YEAR.

10 THE ASIAN **VAMPIRE MOTH** SOMETIMES DRINKS THE BLOOD OF ANIMALS.

7 ROYALTY IN ANCIENT CHINA WORE **BURIAL SUITS** MADE OF **JADE** BECAUSE THEY BELIEVED THE MINERAL WOULD HELP PRESERVE THEIR BODIES.

8 SOME **MONKEYS** IN THAILAND TEACH THEIR YOUNG TO **FLOSS.**

9 PEOPLE ONCE WERE **FINED** IN SINGAPORE FOR **NOT FLUSHING** PUBLIC TOILETS.

PANDA PARTY

CAN WE COME?

NICE PAD!

GIANT PANDAS MOVE INTO A NEW HOME AFTER A DEVASTATING EARTHQUAKE.

Bai Xue the giant panda is ready for her road trip. Bamboo snacks? Check. Comfy cage? Check. Car games? Well, maybe not. But Bai Xue and 17 of her giant panda pals are all set for their journey to their new home.

The animals were traveling to the newly opened China Conservation and Research Center for the Giant Panda in Gengda, China. The drive there took four hours—but the road to find a permanent home has taken four *years*.

That journey started on May 12, 2008, when a powerful earthquake struck southwest China. In two minutes, entire mountainsides sheared off, destroying villages, roads, bamboo forests—and Bai Xue's original home at the research center's base near Chengdu. Staff members made eight daring drives— zigzagging through steep valleys, dodging landslides, and climbing two 13,000-foot-high mountain passes—to transfer 60 pandas to a safe location.

BAMBOOZLED

It's not unusual for scientists to go to such great lengths (and heights!) to save endangered giant pandas. They're especially adored in their homeland of China. Pandas appear in Chinese art dating back thousands of years, and today they're protected under Chinese law.

But development has greatly reduced the panda's habitat and primary food source—bamboo—in the high-elevation forests of southwest China. The giant panda population has fragmented into isolated groups, leaving fewer than 2,000 pandas in the wild. China now has about 50 protected reserves to ensure giant pandas have enough bamboo to eat and safe places to breed.

The new state-of-the-art center in Gengda, which opened in October 2012, has room for more than a hundred pandas. In the nursery section, panda moms and human caregivers take care of newborns. When a cub is a year old

and ready to leave its mother, it moves into a sort of panda kindergarten. There it learns how to find food and explore new environments so that it can one day be released into the wild.

HOME SWEET HOME

The four-hour trip to the new center was a bit of a bumpy ride for Bai Xue and her friends because the road was still undergoing repairs from all the earthquake damage four years ago. The staff secured the pandas' cages to smooth out the ride—and prevent the pandas from getting carsick. A vet rode along to keep an eye out for queasy pandas and pass out treats of bamboo shoots and carrots.

The destination was well worth the journey. The pandas have settled into their new home and spend time climbing trees, play-wrestling, and eating bamboo. In fact, they spend half their day—more than 12 hours!—just eating. Hmm...now where did those snacks go?

GIANT PANDAS CAN SWIFTLY SCALE FIR TREES AS TALL AS 75 FEET.

KEEPERS FEED CARROTS TO GIANT PANDAS AT THE NEW CENTER.

GIANT PANDAS AT THEIR OLD HOME BEFORE THE EARTHQUAKE.

PANDA DROPPINGS CAN BE MADE INTO PAPER.

A PANDA CAN DEVOUR NEARLY **40** POUNDS OF BAMBOO EACH DAY.

MORE ANIMALS OF ASIA

THIS GUY REALLY EARNED HIS STRIPES.

BENGAL TIGER

Bengal tigers don't need to show a passport, only their stripes as they freely cross the border between India and Nepal on the two-mile-long Khata Wildlife Corridor. For the past decade, this stretch of protected grassland has connected two tiger preserves and enabled these endangered cats to roam more safely throughout their range. As a result, the tiger population in the Nepali preserve doubled in two years. Tigers need good news like that: Because of habitat loss and poaching, only about 2,500 Bengal tigers remain. Conservationists are planning to open up more corridors like Khata, in the hopes that one day they might see bumper-to-bumper tigers along those routes.

A TIGER'S SKIN IS STRIPED LIKE ITS FUR.

ASIAN SMALL-CLAWED OTTER

It may be the smallest otter species, but the Asian small-clawed otter is not short on smarts. These creatures have come up with their own version of the microwave. After they pry clams out of the mud and from under rocks, the otters bring the closed clams ashore and let them warm up in the sun. When the shells open up—*ding!*—it's feast time. Then it's playtime. These social creatures—found in rivers from India to the Philippines—are often spotted playing with their siblings along the shore and sliding down muddy banks into the water below.

ASIAN SMALL-CLAWED OTTERS HAVE PARTIALLY WEBBED TOES.

YOU "OTTER" SEE THIS!

REAL-LIFE DRAGON!

KOMODO DRAGON

Don't mess with the Komodo dragon. The world's largest living lizard—measuring up to ten feet long—is a dangerous predator, with about 60 razor-sharp teeth and toxic saliva that can kill with one bite. The lizard's long, yellow tongue can pick up the scent of prey from a mile away, and it can swim from island to island in its Indonesia home. The Komodo dragon is not a picky eater: Water buffalo, snakes, deer, and even young Komodos are on the menu. No wonder the youngsters spend their first four years up in trees.

THE KOMODO DRAGON CAN RUN AS FAST AS A HUMAN FOR SHORT DISTANCES.

A GROUP OF PEACOCKS IS CALLED A PARTY.

INDIAN PEACOCK

The "eyes" have it when it comes to peacocks. That's because peacocks with the most eyespots in their blue, green, and gold tail feathers tend to have the best luck impressing females, called peahens. It's not just a matter of style. Peacocks with more eyespots, called ocelli, have stronger immune systems, a trait that peahens would want to pass on to their chicks. But the females' dull feathers also can be an advantage. The drab plumage helps peahens hide in the brush, evading predators such as tigers and leopards in the forests of India, Sri Lanka, Pakistan, and Nepal.

WHAT A GREAT APE!

SUMATRAN ORANGUTAN

How can you spot a healthy old orangutan? Check out his hair! If he has a full head of long, fine, red hair, and if the cheek pads around his face are firm, then grandpa is holding up well. Unfortunately, the critically endangered Sumatran orangutan faces far greater threats than baldness. These huge apes—which can measure up to 6 feet tall and 200 pounds—spend nearly their entire lives up in the trees. But deforestation has destroyed much of the orangutan's habitat on the Indonesian island of Sumatra. Conservation and government officials are now trying to protect the orangutans' forests so that these apes can survive to have another great hair day.

CLEVER ORANGUTANS HAVE BEEN KNOWN TO PADDLE STOLEN CANOES, UNLOCK DOORS WITH HOMEMADE KEYS, AND LEARN HOW TO WHISTLE.

71

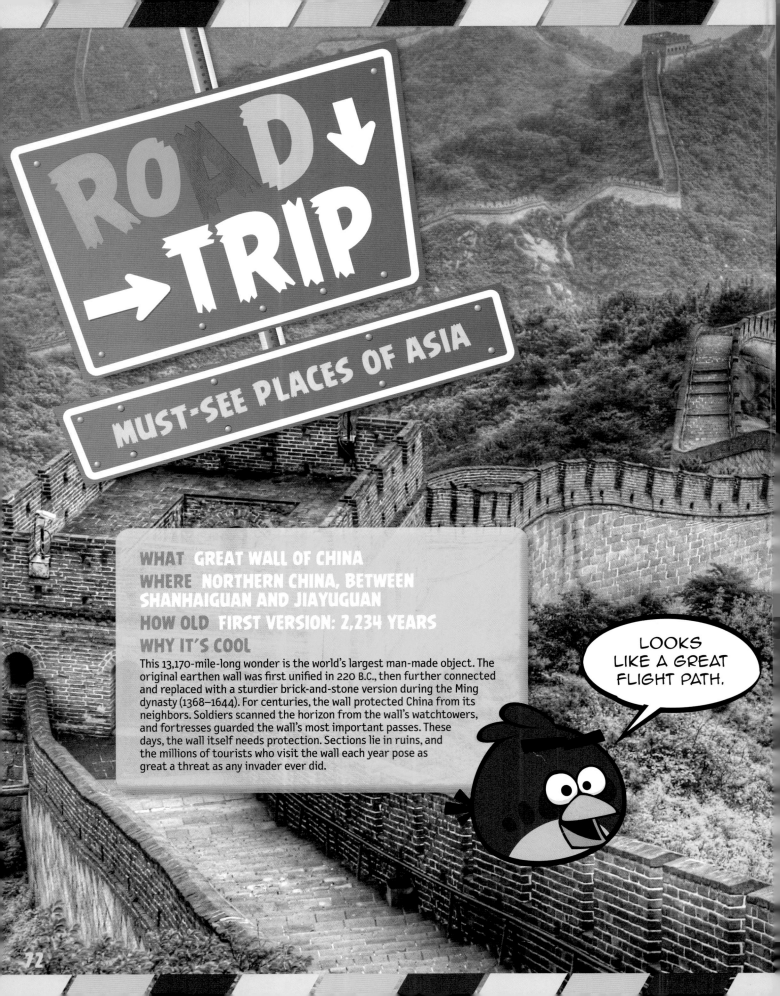

ROAD TRIP

MUST-SEE PLACES OF ASIA

WHAT GREAT WALL OF CHINA

WHERE NORTHERN CHINA, BETWEEN SHANHAIGUAN AND JIAYUGUAN

HOW OLD FIRST VERSION: 2,234 YEARS

WHY IT'S COOL

This 13,170-mile-long wonder is the world's largest man-made object. The original earthen wall was first unified in 220 B.C., then further connected and replaced with a sturdier brick-and-stone version during the Ming dynasty (1368–1644). For centuries, the wall protected China from its neighbors. Soldiers scanned the horizon from the wall's watchtowers, and fortresses guarded the wall's most important passes. These days, the wall itself needs protection. Sections lie in ruins, and the millions of tourists who visit the wall each year pose as great a threat as any invader ever did.

> LOOKS LIKE A GREAT FLIGHT PATH.

I ALWAYS SAY THAT THREE HEADS ARE BETTER THAN ONE.

WHAT ERAWAN MUSEUM
WHERE SAMUT PRAKAN, THAILAND
HOW OLD 10 YEARS
WHY IT'S COOL

Elephants are supposed to have great memories, but *you'll* never forget this three-headed elephant towering 144 feet high just outside Bangkok. Designed to resemble the Hindu elephant god Erawan, the structure is actually a museum of Southeast Asian antiques. An elaborate staircase carries visitors up into the elephant's belly and through three levels of opulent carvings, ancient statues, and soaring columns.

WHAT TAJ MAHAL
WHERE AGRA, INDIA
HOW OLD 366 YEARS
WHY IT'S COOL

Most guys just give candy or flowers to show their affection. Shah Jahan—a powerful ruler in the 1600s—went much further, creating one of the world's most beautiful buildings as a tomb for his beloved dead wife. It's said that 20,000 laborers toiled to build this stunning white marble mausoleum, which took 17 years to create. Up to four million visitors each year stroll past the enormous reflecting pool and under the monument's 240-foot dome. Unfortunately, Shah Jahan was unable to visit his wife's tomb toward the end of his own life—his son imprisoned him!

WHAT ANGKOR ARCHAEOLOGICAL PARK
WHERE SIEM REAP PROVINCE, CAMBODIA
HOW OLD MORE THAN 1,100 YEARS
WHY IT'S COOL

Hidden in a forest, the ancient stone city of Angkor was the seat of the Khmer Empire for more than 500 years, between the 9th and 15th centuries. The complex stretches over an area roughly the size of New York City and contains more stones than the Pyramids at Giza. Many of those stones were moved to the site by an elaborate system of canals, which also provided water for the 750,000 residents, as well as for crops. In the 15th century, the city was mysteriously abandoned. No one—including scientists—has been able to figure out why.

73

HIGH NOTE

FOR ONE TEEN, PLAYING AN ANCIENT MUSICAL INSTRUMENT KEEPS HIS CULTURE ALIVE.

TWEET!

Txhim Thoj keeps going around in circles. Don't worry: He's not lost or confused. Instead, this teenager from a small village near Sapa, Vietnam, is practicing the moves that musicians perform while playing the *qeej*, an ancient musical instrument that's an important part of the Hmong culture.

The Hmong (pronounced MONG) people have left their footprints all over eastern Asia—literally. For the past 5,000 years, they've migrated south from Mongolia and through China before establishing small farming communities in the mountains of Thailand, Laos, and Vietnam. While dress and dialects may differ from place to place, the qeej (pronounced CANE) is part of community life for all Hmong. "The qeej has been kept alive by the Hmong people for a long time," says Txhim (pronounced SEE). "It's good that we continue this tradition."

The qeej is an L-shaped bamboo-and-wood mouth organ. It has six pipes of different lengths attached to a wooden air chamber. Picture playing a recorder: The musician blows into the chamber and covers up holes in the pipes with his fingers to produce sounds that are a cross between an organ and bagpipes. "Making the different notes is difficult," Txhim says. "You need to use several different finger positions to make one note."

Txhim belongs to a group called Hmong Leng. Unlike most of his peers, he lives and studies away from home during the week at his boarding school, Sapa O'Chau. When he comes back home, he practices the qeej with his oldest brother,

Chu. Sometimes he plays the instrument with the village qeej master.

Qeej players dance in circles because they believe that it confuses evil spirits that might be attracted by the music. Txhim, however, hopes that his qeej playing will attract an entirely different audience. "I want to become a master qeej player so that everyone will know who I am," he says. "Then I will be given gifts of buffalo meat and meet many beautiful girls."

PLAYING THE *QEEJ*

HMONG OFTEN GROW RICE AND CORN IN FIELDS LIKE THESE.

GLAD I CAN FLY INSTEAD OF WALK UP THAT HILL!

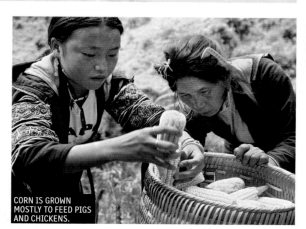
CORN IS GROWN MOSTLY TO FEED PIGS AND CHICKENS.

> BET WE WOULD SOUND AWESOME TOGETHER.

HOLDING HIS *QEEJ*, TXHIM WEARS CLOTHES HANDMADE BY HIS FAMILY.

HOW WOULD YOUR LIFE BE DIFFERENT...
IF YOU WERE TRADITIONAL HMONG LENG?

FOOD	rice and vegetables, sometimes with chicken or pork; water buffalo meat on special occasions
HOUSE	bamboo, thatched, or wooden house with a beaten-earth floor, with palm leaves for the roof and a fireplace for cooking and heat (but no chimney)
CHORES	**Boys:** tend animals, fish, hunt for birds. **Girls:** babysit younger siblings, cook, clean. **Both:** help with farming, collect firewood
CLOTHING	**Boys:** long black pants and a vest, often with a long-sleeve white shirt and colorful sash. **Girls:** embroidered long-sleeve tunic paired with a skirt, sometimes with pants or leg warmers underneath; often a scarf or hat as a head covering
FOR FUN	**Boys:** *tuj lub* (pronounced THU-LOO), a spinning-top game; playing the flute or *qeej*. **Girls:** embroidery; playing the *ncas* (pronounced ING-YAH), a mouth harp

START THE PARTY, ASIA STYLE!

HOLI
INDIA
Duck! On second thought, don't—getting pelted by colored powder is part of the fun during this Hindu festival that celebrates spring. After a bonfire, celebrants chase each other through the streets to throw water and brilliantly colored powders so that everyone becomes a walking rainbow.

DRAGON BOAT FESTIVAL
CHINA, MALAYSIA, SINGAPORE
No fire breathing here, just heated competition as teams of 20 to 22 rowers try to cross the finish line first in their fierce-looking dragon boats. These festivals, usually held in June, honor a Chinese hero from 2,300 years ago. A drummer aboard each vessel pounds out a rhythm.

CAMEL BEAUTY PAGEANT
MADINAT ZAYID, UNITED ARAB EMIRATES
Beauty really is in the eye of the beholder. In the eyes of the judges evaluating the 24,000 camels competing for top honors at this December pageant, nothing is more attractive than firm ears, a dangling bottom lip, and a high and symmetrical hump. Maybe there's a talent competition too.

MARKET MIX-UP

The Angry Birds are amazed by all the goods at Damnoen Saduak Floating Market in Thailand. But some of the items are in the wrong place. Match each of the 15 numbered spaces to its missing item. For instance, number one shows a missing postcard, which has been misplaced on a boat. **ANSWERS ON PAGE 103**

THINK I COULD PULL OFF ONE OF THESE HATS?

WELCOME TO AUSTRALIA

WE COME TO A LAND DOWN UNDER!

G'DAY, MATE! THAT MEANS "HELLO, FRIEND!" IN AUSTRALIA,

a continent where most people speak English...but you might not understand them. "How ya going?" actually means "How are you doing?" A "jumper" is a sweater, "strides" are pants, "chocky" means chocolate, and "sanger" is a sandwich.

Language is just one thing that sets apart Earth's smallest continent from the rest of the world. The koala, platypus, and wombat are found only in Australia, as are 20 of the 25 most venomous snakes. (Yikes!) But Australia is also a land of striking contrasts. The enormous sandstone monolith named Uluru dramatically changes color—from dusty brown to glowing red—against the surrounding barren landscape. And though about 18 percent of Australia is desert, the 1,429-mile-long Great Barrier Reef is home to more than 1,500 species of fish and 400 varieties of colorful coral.

Australia's Aboriginal people—the world's oldest living culture—have lived on the continent for 50,000 years, but the first Western explorers and settlers arrived only in the late 1700s. Many came against their will—as prisoners! For a hundred years, British authorities sent convicts from England, Ireland, Scotland, and Wales to this isolated island. Today about 20 percent of Australians are descended from those inmates. But all Australians proudly share a strong spirit of respect and loyalty—known as "mateship"—throughout this land down under.

AUSTRALIA FACTS

LAND AREA
2,968,000 square miles

NUMBER OF COUNTRIES
14 (includes surrounding island nations)

POPULATION
36,620,000

LARGEST METROPOLITAN AREA
Sydney, Australia
(4,543,000 people)

LARGEST LAKE
Lake Eyre
(3,741 square miles)

LARGEST COUNTRY
Australia
(2,969,906 square miles)

DENSEST COUNTRY
Nauru (1,256 people per square mile)

LONGEST RIVER
Murray (1,476 miles)

HIGHEST POINT
Mount Kosciuszko, Australia (7,310 feet)

LOOK OUT FOR THAT BOOMERANG!

AUSTRALIA

NEXT 5km

20 COOL THINGS

1 "GOOG" IS ANOTHER NAME FOR EGG IN AUSTRALIA.

2 ONE TYPE OF AUSTRALIAN **FLOWER** SPENDS ITS ENTIRE LIFE UNDERGROUND.

3 JANUARY AND FEBRUARY ARE THE WARMEST MONTHS IN AUSTRALIA, WHILE JUNE AND JULY ARE THE COLDEST.

4 **VENOM** FROM THE AGGRESSIVE SYDNEY FUNNEL-WEB SPIDER CAN KILL A HUMAN IN AN HOUR.

5 AUSTRALIA WAS ONCE A BRITISH PRISON COLONY.

6 AUSTRALIA'S **ABORIGINAL PEOPLE** HAVE MAPPED THEIR OWN STAR CONSTELLATIONS.

7 MALE PLATYPUSES ARE **VENOMOUS.**

14 SEABIRDS OFTEN PERCH ON THE BACKS OF FLOATING **FLATBACK SEA TURTLES.**

15 IN CANBERRA, AUSTRALIA, THOUSANDS OF **EASTERN GRAY KANGAROOS** OFTEN INVADE THE CITY TO DRINK WATER AND MUNCH GRASS.

16 THE **LITTLE PENGUIN** IS THE SIZE OF A **FOOTBALL...AND BLUE-GRAY.**

MAYBE I'LL TRY PERCHING ON A SEA TURTLE.

LOVE THE BLUE FEATHERS.

ABOUT AUSTRALIA

17 THE **OPAL** IS AUSTRALIA'S **NATIONAL GEMSTONE.**

18 IN SOME REMOTE AREAS, AIRPLANES DOUBLE AS **AMBULANCES.**

19 TASMANIAN DEVILS LIVE ON THE AUSTRALIAN ISLAND OF **TASMANIA.**

13 ORIGINALLY FROM AUSTRALIA, **BOOMERANGS** HAVE BEEN USED FOR **HUNTING** AND IN **SPORTING** EVENTS FOR THOUSANDS OF YEARS.

20 ON AUSTRALIA'S **CHRISTMAS ISLAND,** NEARLY 50 MILLION **RED CRABS** SCURRY TO THE BEACHES ONCE A YEAR TO MATE.

12 USING A METAL DETECTOR, AN AUSTRALIAN MAN FOUND A **60-POUND GOLD NUGGET** NEAR A SCHOOL.

11 **GHOST BATS** ARE ONE OF THE ONLY BATS WITH **WHITE FUR.**

8 A RABBITLIKE MAMMAL CALLED A **BILBY** IS THE EASTER "BUNNY" FOR PEOPLE IN AUSTRALIA.

9 **ONE TIME ZONE** IN AUSTRALIA HAS ONLY **ABOUT 200** PEOPLE IN IT.

10 MEN AND WOMEN WHO WORK ON LARGE FARMS ARE CALLED **JACKAROOS** **AND JILLAROOS.**

KOALA CAPER

A CLEVER KOALA HITCHES A RIDE TO SHOW IT'S MORE THAN JUST A SLEEPY TREE DWELLER.

To the canoers, the koala on the bank of Talle-budgera Creek in Queensland, Australia, was a cute photo op. But to the koala, the huge outrigger canoe was a ride it couldn't resist. It leaped into the water and koala-paddled straight toward the boat.

"I couldn't believe it," says paddler Julie Elliott of the Burleigh Point Outrigger Canoe Club. "I've been paddling on the creek for a good ten years, and I've never encountered anything like this."

The daring koala quickly tired out during its 50-foot swim. "Its coat was getting so heavy with water," Elliott says. "It scratched at the side of the boat, so we pulled it into the canoe." As Elliott stood up, the marsupial plopped down on her seat. "It was totally mellow," she says.

UP A CREEK

No one is sure why the koala decided to hitch a ride in the canoe. Koalas aren't usually seen in the water and in fact spend most of their time—between 18 and 22 hours a day—sleeping in eucalyptus trees. But lately encounters between koalas and humans have become more frequent, and sometimes dangerous.

Not too long ago, millions of koalas thrived in Australian forests. Then people moved in, cutting down trees to build roads, houses, factories, and malls. Koalas need a lot of space: about a hundred trees per animal. Development has squeezed and fragmented their turf in eastern and south-eastern Australia, forcing them to cross roads, scale fences, travel greater distances, and face bigger dangers as they move from one eucalyptus feast to the next.

Conservationists are working all over Australia to protect koala habitat, and "koala hospitals" have popped up to help the marsupials injured by cars, dogs, and other dangerous encounters. Those hospitals hope to return the koalas back to the wild—and back into their beloved eucalyptus trees.

TREE HOUSE

A koala's compact body is perfectly designed for its arboreal lifestyle. Its curved spine and rounded rear end enable it to curl up more easily on branches. Their front paws have two opposable thumbs, giving them a tighter grip as they climb. At night they chow down on about two pounds of eucalyptus leaves, which provide both the food and water they need to survive. In fact, the name koala comes from the Aboriginal term meaning "no drink."

The koala seemed to enjoy its brief time in the canoe. "It was as if it were saying, 'All right, where are you taking me?'" Elliott says. But the canoers knew human contact wasn't good for the koala and quickly returned it to the creek bank. They did bestow their visitor with an honorary name, however: Kanu the Koala.

LIKE MOST MARSUPIALS, THE KOALA CARRIES ITS YOUNG IN A POUCH FOR ABOUT SIX MONTHS.

MORE ANIMALS OF AUSTRALIA

GREAT WHITE SHARK

The great white shark may have been named for its white underbelly, but its serrated, triangular pearly whites—as many as 300 of them—have helped this powerful predator earn its fearsome reputation. Found in coastal waters around the world, it prowls Australia's coasts in search of seals as well as young and feeble humpback whales. It can detect tiny electrical charges given off by prey, and its extremely sensitive nose can sniff out traces of blood as far as three miles away—a distance this torpedo-shaped shark can cover in no time.

LIKE ALL SHARKS, GREAT WHITES HAVE NO BONES.

HOP TO IT!

RED KANGAROO

Why do kangaroos hop? Because they can't walk. A red kangaroo's legs cannot move independently, so instead the world's largest marsupial bounces along Australia's deserts and grasslands at speeds up to 35 miles an hour. In fact, they can cover 25 feet in a single bound. (Take *that*, Superman!) The blue-tinged females are smaller, lighter, and faster, so Australians have nicknamed them "blue fliers." Males, called boomers, compete for fliers by "boxing." They lean back on their strong tails, hit each other with their front paws, and kick one another with their powerful hind legs.

KANGAROOS DON'T HOP BACKWARD.

COMMON WOMBAT

Don't even think about butting into a common wombat's burrow. This short, stocky marsupial uses its thick-skinned rump to block intruders from entering its home. These expert diggers from southeastern Australia prefer to live alone, yet they scoop out underground tunnels that can stretch for 650 feet and easily fit 260 wombats, nose to tail. But joeys don't need to worry about a dirt shower while mom digs—her pouch opens to the rear. These critters are so at home underground that it's hard to imagine that their rhinoceros-size ancestor, the giant wombat, roamed the Australian plains 50,000 years ago.

A WOMBAT'S FRONT TEETH NEVER STOP GROWING.

WE COULD BE QUADRUPLETS.

CASSOWARY

Who you calling hairy? This peculiar-looking flightless bird seems like it's covered in black hair. With a closer look, you'll see fluffy black feathers, which shield it from thorns and keep it dry in its rain forest habitat of northern Australia and New Guinea. Just don't get too close. The cassowary is considered one of the more dangerous birds in the world. Its dagger-like claws can slice open any predator with a single kick. Hmm... forget hairy. *Scary* is more like it!

THE CASSOWARY CAN GROW TO BE SIX FEET TALL.

FRESHWATER CROCODILE

A shy crocodile? If you're talking about "freshies," which is what Aussies call the freshwater crocs that live only in northern Australia's inland rivers, the answer is yes! These timid creatures leave their eggs unattended on sandbars, but mothers return to their nests on hatching day to carry hatchlings in their mouths to the water. Freshies have shorter bodies than their saltwater cousins (called "salties") and hunt smaller prey such as bats, birds, and fish with a sudden sideways snap of their narrower snout. OK, maybe they're not *that* shy.

CROCODILES CAN'T CHEW.

ROAD TRIP

MUST-SEE PLACES OF AUSTRALIA

WHAT ULURU
WHERE ULURU, NORTHERN TERRITORIES
HOW OLD SOME 535 TO 550 MILLION YEARS
WHY IT'S COOL

At sunrise and sunset, this 1,142-foot-high red sandstone monolith glows against the stark landscape of Australia's central plains. Take a ranger-led walk around the nearly 6.5-mile base of Uluru, which is considered sacred by the Anangu Aboriginal people. You'll learn about the rock art that's tens of thousands of years old and the fascinating stories the pictures tell about spirits such as the poisonous snake man and the python woman. Temperatures at Uluru can reach 116°F in the summer, so start your hike early and bring lots of water!

WHAT LARRY THE LOBSTER
WHERE KINGSTON, AUSTRALIA
HOW OLD 35 YEARS
WHY IT'S COOL

This ginormous spiny lobster statue along Australia's southern coast looks good enough to eat. Designer Paul Kelly modeled Larry the Lobster—as it's known by locals—after a real lobster he bought. Kelly spent six months building the 56-foot-tall crustacean out of steel and fiberglass. Since Larry would be mighty tough on the teeth, visitors may want to order the real thing at the accompanying seafood restaurant instead.

DON'T FLY TOO CLOSE TO THAT GUY.

WHERE'S THE PARROT FISH?

WHAT GREAT BARRIER REEF
WHERE STRETCHES FOR 1,429 MILES ALONG THE NORTHEAST COAST OF AUSTRALIA
HOW OLD 500,000 YEARS, THOUGH PRESENT REEF STRUCTURE IS ABOUT 6,000 TO 8,000 YEARS OLD
WHY IT'S COOL

This is the greatest underwater show on Earth. More than 1,500 species of fish—ranging from the whale shark to the clownfish—make their home among the world's most extensive reef ecosystem, which stretches nearly the same distance as from Miami, Florida, to New York City. Dive in for a closer look at the 400 varieties of colorful coral, from frilly fans to gnarly knobs. Dugongs—known as sea cows—and many sea turtle species feast on the reef's buffet of sea grass.

WHAT SYDNEY OPERA HOUSE
WHERE SYDNEY, AUSTRALIA
HOW OLD 41 YEARS
WHY IT'S COOL

This gleaming white architectural marvel overlooks Sydney Harbor and was designed to look like a ship at full sail. The builders projected this concert hall would take four years and $7.25 million to complete. Um, not quite! Fourteen years and $105 million later, this grand venue finally opened its doors in 1973. But it seems to have been worth the wait—more than 8.2 million people visit the site each year.

THAT IS ONE BIG ROCK.

FAMILY PORTRAIT

AUSTRALIA IS AWESOME!

THE ABORIGINALS OF AUSTRALIA TRACE HISTORY THROUGH AMAZING BODY PAINTINGS.

The girl sits very still, her eyes closed. An elder leans over and carefully dabs colorful dots—yellow, white, red, and black—across the girl's cheeks and nose. The pattern could represent several things: wild honey, a stringy gum bark tree, a fire. With one look, fellow members of the girl's clan—her extended family group—can connect the dots and recognize which ancient story is now written across the girl's face.

Aboriginal people don't trace their history in Australia in years (50,000 of them!). They trace them in stories and art about the Dreaming, or Dreamtime, when they believe that ancestral beings created the world. Their paintings—whether on rocks, canvas, or their bodies—help keep those stories and spirits alive and are part of any important ceremony.

Today more than half a million Aboriginals live just like most people do all over Australia. But they usually identify themselves with their particular clan. "Each clan has its own unique paintings, tied to its land and its myths," says Howard Morphy, an expert on Aboriginal art. "These designs are part of the clan's heritage. They can only be painted by someone who has permission."

Young children usually start out covering their bodies in white clay or red ocher. "The paintings are signs of respect, like they're 'dressing' in a proper way for a ceremony," Morphy says. After initiation ceremonies when they're around six to eight, kids begin to wear more elaborate designs painted on by elders. Perhaps if this girl listens as the elders share their stories, one day she'll graduate from "painted" to painter and help keep the Dreaming alive.

THE BODY ART HERE REPRESENTS VINES.

AN ABORIGINAL WOMAN TEACHES CHILDREN TRADITIONAL DANCE.

THIS LOOKS LIKE FUN.

GEOMETRIC BODY ART DESIGNS CAN HAVE SEVERAL MEANINGS. FOR INSTANCE, THIS PATTERN COULD BE ASSOCIATED WITH WILD HONEY OR THE STRINGY GUM BARK TREE.

HOW COOL!

BIRDMAN RALLY
MELBOURNE, AUSTRALIA

Birdbrains of a feather flock together to see if they really can fly at this amusing March festival. Here, costumed competitors leap off a platform into a pool. "Hawks" try to fly the farthest, while "penguins" win points for creativity.

AUSTRALIAN SAND SCULPTING CHAMPIONSHIPS

SURFERS PARADISE, AUSTRALIA

With more than 15,000 miles of coastline, Australia definitely has plenty of sand to sculpt. This February competition transforms one of Queensland's most popular beaches into a golden gallery, where sculptors mold and carve over 70 tons of sand into things such as castles, pirates, and snorkelers.

DREAMING FESTIVAL
WOODFORD, AUSTRALIA

You'll definitely want to be awake for this year-end, six-day celebration of indigenous cultures from around the world. Performers sing, dance, and share plays and art that celebrate their cultural traditions.

HOW WOULD YOUR LIFE BE DIFFERENT IF YOU WERE AN ABORIGINAL KID IN SOUTHEASTERN AUSTRALIA IN THE 1830s?

FOOD	kangaroo or possum meat, eels, yams, orchid or water lily roots
HOUSE	Temporary shelters made of tree branches. Eel trappers built more substantial houses with stone walls and a thatched roof.
CHORES	gather and prepare food, collect firewood and water, tend the fire, spin plant fiber into string
CLOTHING	Sometimes a loincloth. In winter, possum skins were pinned together with wood toggles for cloaks.
FOR FUN	swimming, dancing, making string figures, playing kickball with a ball of opossum fur bound with kangaroo sinew

DOWN UNDERWATER

These two scenes in the Great Barrier Reef may seem the same, but there are actually at least 20 differences between them. Find and circle the differences. (The Angry Birds and the borders don't count!) **ANSWERS ON PAGE 103**

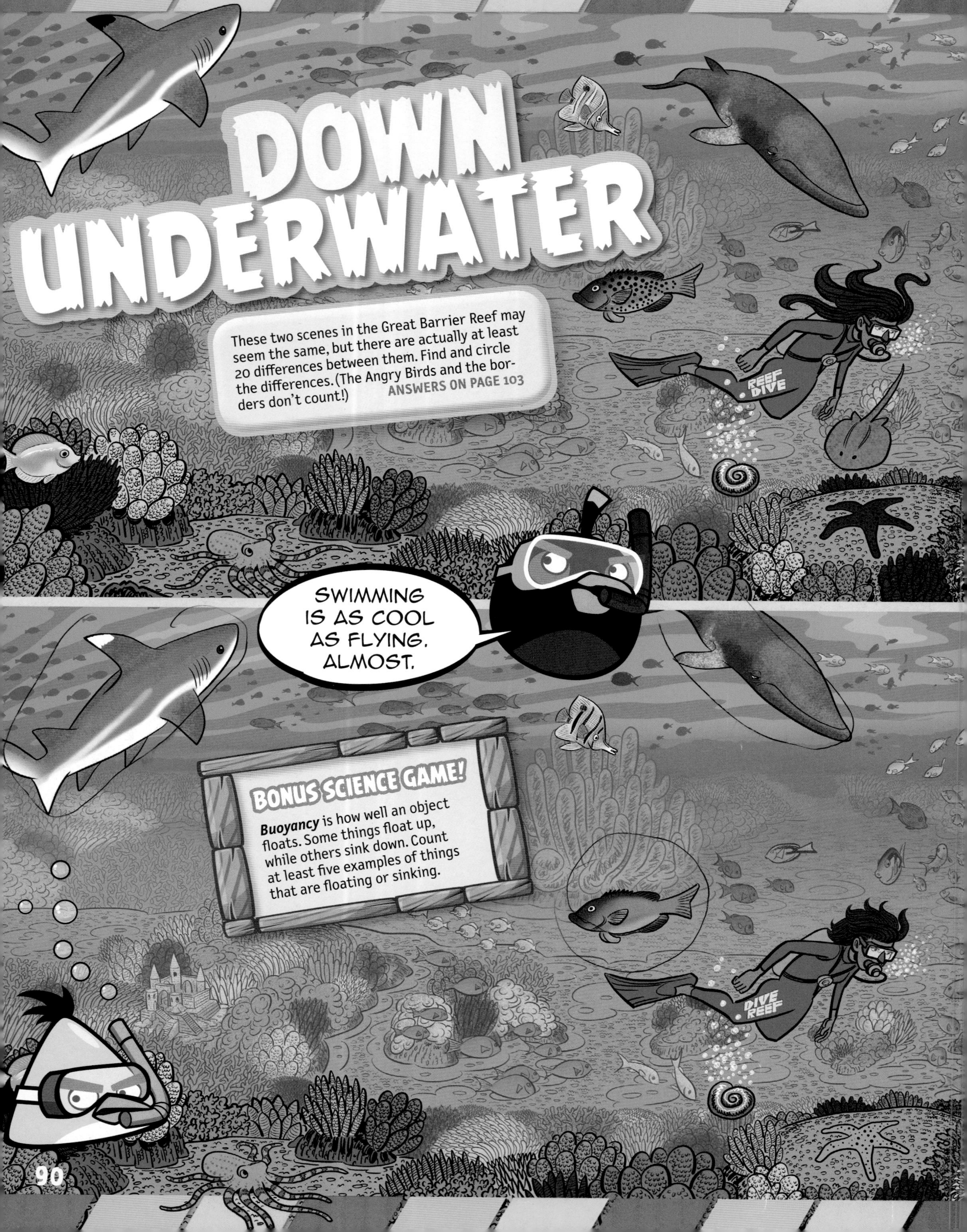

SWIMMING IS AS COOL AS FLYING. ALMOST.

BONUS SCIENCE GAME!

Buoyancy is how well an object floats. Some things float up, while others sink down. Count at least five examples of things that are floating or sinking.

REEF DIVE

DIVE REEF

WELCOME TO ANTARCTICA

LAST STOP!

WITH WINTER TEMPERATURES THAT CAN DROP TO MINUS 73°F AND WIND GUSTS UP TO 200 MILES AN HOUR,

it's teeth-chatteringly clear why the continent of Antarctica doesn't have any permanent human residents. In fact, no country owns Antarctica. Instead dozens of countries work together to study and care for its barren landscape.

And so, every year some 3,500 hardy individuals from around the world bundle up for short-term summer stints at the research stations scattered across the coldest, windiest, and driest continent of all. ("Summer" on the coasts means close to freezing.) Many are scientists who study everything from ancient ice to volcanic Mount Erebus, which spews out about two-tenths of a pound of gold every time it erupts. Others work as support staff, including cooks, carpenters, and firefighters. All of them must take a survival course that prepares them for their frigid fieldwork.

Antarctica's animals far outnumber the humans who come to study them. Colonies of emperor penguins live here year-round. Other animals, such as the humpback whale and the arctic tern, are just visitors. Like the scientists, they, too, will one day leave this icy land for someplace warmer. Much warmer!

ANTARCTICA FACTS

LAND AREA
5,100,000 square miles

HIGHEST POINT
Vinson Massif (16,066 feet)

LOWEST POINT
Bentley Subglacial (-8,383 feet)

LOWEST RECORDED TEMPERATURE
Vostok Research Station, Russia (-128.6°F)

HIGHEST RECORDED TEMPERATURE
Vanda Research Station, New Zealand (currently closed) (59°F)

COLDEST PLACE ON EARTH
Ridge A (annual average temperature -94°F)

1

MOST FISH HERE HAVE NATURAL "ANTIFREEZE" IN THEIR BLOOD.

2

A KETCHUP BOTTLE FROM 1912 IS IN AN OLD EXPLORER'S CABIN.

3

SCIENTISTS HAVE RETRIEVED **800,000-YEAR-OLD** ANTARCTIC ICE.

4

ALL **WATER** AT THE **SOUTH POLE** IS MELTED ICE.

5

ONE GIANT ICEBERG WAS NEARLY THE SIZE OF CONNECTICUT.

16

NO DOGS ARE ALLOWED IN **ANTARCTICA.**

17

TWO **26-MILE RACES** ARE HELD EACH YEAR ON THIS ICY CONTINENT.

18

THE ANTARCTIC **FUR SEAL** CAN SPEND **WEEKS AT SEA** EATING FISH, SQUID, AND EVEN BIRDS.

6

THE **LOWEST** TEMPERATURE ON EARTH (-128.6°F) WAS RECORDED IN ANTARCTICA.

7

ANTARCTICA WAS LOCATED NEAR THE **EQUATOR** HUNDREDS OF MILLIONS OF YEARS AGO.

8

WINDS HERE CAN GUST AT MORE THAN **200 MILES** AN HOUR.

ABOUT ANTARCTICA

15 SCIENTISTS VISITING THE CONTINENT MUST TAKE A SURVIVAL COURSE CALLED "HAPPY CAMPER SCHOOL."

14 THE LARGEST **LAND-ONLY ANIMAL** IN ANTARCTICA IS A WINGLESS **INSECT** CALLED A MIDGE.

13 A VOLCANO CALLED MOUNT EREBUS OCCASIONALLY SPEWS 10-FOOT-WIDE **LAVA BOMBS.**

12 ANTARCTICA CAN HAVE **24 HOURS** OF DAYLIGHT IN SUMMER.

OPEN WIDE!

19 **ELEPHANT SEALS** LIVING ALONG THE COAST CAN **STAY UNDERWATER** FOR UP TO **TWO HOURS.**

20 THE **"BANANA BELT"** IS A GROUP OF NEARBY ISLANDS WHERE **SUMMER TEMPERATURES** STAY ABOVE FREEZING.

THEN HOW AM I SUPPOSED TO BUILD A SNOWMAN?

9 THE **SOUTH POLE** GETS ONLY ABOUT **ONE INCH OF SNOW** A YEAR.

10 IT HASN'T **RAINED** FOR AT LEAST **800,000** YEARS IN PARTS OF THIS CONTINENT.

11 THERE ARE TWO **ATMs** IN ANTARCTICA.

ANIMALS OF ANTARCTICA

EMPEROR PENGUIN

Emperor penguins just might win the Parent of the Year Award. Both mom and dad emperor penguins go through tremendous hardships to care for their offspring in the brutally cold Antarctic landscape. Once she lays her single egg, the mother leaves on a fishing trip that can last two months and take her as far as 100 miles away to find the fish, squid, and krill to sustain her family. Back on the ice, the father balances the egg on top of his feet and then stands there, without food, in windchills down to minus 76°F. The chick hatches in about 64 days. Too bad there's no takeout on Antarctica.

HEY GUYS, HOW ABOUT A NICE RED BOW TIE?

WAIT TILL HE SEES OUR BACKSTROKE!

LEOPARD SEAL

The leopard seal shares more with its namesake than just its spotted coat. They're both fierce predators that ambush prey and attack with powerful jaws. These streamlined seals can race through the water at 25 miles an hour, but they're just as likely to be patiently hanging out under the ice, waiting for tasty penguins to jump in. The females outgrow the males, weighing about 1,000 pounds and measuring over 13 feet in length. These solitary creatures spread out over millions of miles of pack ice. Just try to, um, *spot* one!

ORCA

What do you call a group of orcas? An O-Pod! Up to 40 of these creatures hunt together in a pod for fish, birds, seals, and even whales. Like other dolphins (yep, they're dolphins—the world's largest), orcas use echolocation, bouncing sound waves off objects to determine their prey's location, size, and shape. These intelligent predators also tip over ice floes to topple penguins and seals into the water. With each orca weighing more than 6 tons and measuring about 30 feet long, maybe a group of orcas should be called an XL-Pod instead.

TALK ABOUT A MAMA'S BOY. MALE ORCAS LIVE WITH THEIR MOTHERS FOR MOST OF THEIR LIVES.

NICE HAIRDO!

WANDERING ALBATROSS

Talk about a frequent flier. This hungry wanderer may fly nearly 10,000 miles to deliver one meal to its chick and can rack up nearly 4 million miles over a 50-year life span. Its 11-foot wingspan—the largest of any bird—makes it easy to glide for hours above the Southern Ocean. Unfortunately, this vulnerable species often gets caught accidentally in commercial fishing nets and on hooks. The birds also can choke on plastic trash in the ocean. A change in fishing methods and a new protected reserve are helping clear this bird for takeoff again.

A WANDERING ALBATROSS SOMETIMES DANCES WITH ITS MATE.

MACARONI PENGUIN

It's nearly impossible to miss a group of macaroni penguins. First, there's the penguin's telltale bright-yellow crest. And you'll definitely hear them: Once a male macaroni unleashes its harsh bray to attract a mate, it can spark an earsplitting trumpeting among all the males in the colony. Unfortunately, you'll also smell them! When millions of macaroni penguins gather together in their massive rookeries in Antarctica, their pungent odor can be detected as far as six miles offshore. Smell ya later—much, much later!

MACARONI PENGUINS WERE NAMED AFTER A GROUP OF 18TH-CENTURY BRITISH MEN CALLED MACARONIS WHO WORE WILD WIGS AND FANCY CLOTHES.

ILLUSTRATION CREDITS

GRAND GETAWAY (PAGES 20-21)

BONUS SCIENCE GAME: Things that are moving include the toy helicopter, the Frisbee, and the bald eagle. Things that are storing energy include the golden retriever and the football.

AMAZON ADVENTURE (PAGES 34-35)

BONUS SCIENCE GAME: Examples of friction include the landslide, the sliding backpack, the rolling apple, the rolling jaguar, the sliding river otter, the rolling nut, the rolling table, the sliding cooler, the sliding sock, and the rolling car.

ANSWERS

FREE FALL (PAGES 48-49)

BONUS SCIENCE GAME: Gravity is pulling the following objects to Earth: coins, a hat, birdseed, a lunch bag, sunglasses, an apple, keys, a cup, a drawing, and an ice-cream cone.

GO ON SAFARI (PAGES 62-63)

BONUS SCIENCE GAME: There are 55 curves in the solution.

MARKET MIX-UP (PAGES 76-77)

BONUS SCIENCE GAME: Things that have a lot of mass include the boats, the pots, the paddles, the standing camera, and the turtle vase. Things that have very little mass include the flowers, the napkins, the paper, the pencil, and the feathers.

DOWN UNDERWATER (PAGES 90-91)

BONUS SCIENCE GAME: Examples of floating up include the black-tip shark, the green sea turtle, and the olive sea snake. Examples of sinking down include the snail and the anchor.

CHILLIN' OUT (PAGES 98-99)

BONUS SCIENCE GAME: Examples of force: Scientists are pulling a tent and a box open. Another scientist is pulling an apple from the tree. A scientist is pushing a door open. The alien is pushing his spaceship.

NATIONAL GEOGRAPHIC · **ROVIO LEARNING**

PUBLISHED BY THE NATIONAL GEOGRAPHIC SOCIETY
Gary Knell, *President and CEO*
John M. Fahey, *Chairman of the Board*
Declan Moore, *President, Publishing and Digital Media*
Claudia Malley, *Executive Vice President and Worldwide Publisher*
Finance John J. Patermaster, Jr., *Business Manager*; Cindy Ramroop, *Contract Manager*
Consumer and Member Marketing
Elizabeth Safford, *Vice President*; John MacKethan, *Vice President, Retail Sales*
Publicity Anna Irwin, *Communications Director*; Megan Heltzel, *Publicist* (202) 457-8465

PREPARED BY NATIONAL GEOGRAPHIC KIDS MAGAZINE
Melina Gerosa Bellows, *Chief Creative Officer, Books, Kids, and Family*
Nancy Laties Feresten, *Senior Vice President, Kids Publishing and Media*
Julie Vosburgh Agnone, *Vice President, Editorial Operations*
Rachel Buchholz, *Editor and Vice President*
Eva Absher-Schantz, *Design Director, Kids Publishing and Media*
Jay Sumner, *Photo Director, Kids Publishing and Media*
Rachael Hamm Plett, *Design, Moduza Design*
Kristin Baird Rattini, *Chief Writer*
Michelle Rae Harris, *Researcher*
Catherine D. Hughes, *Senior Editor, Science*

Editorial Andrea Silen, *Associate Editor*; Nick Spagnoli, *Copy Editor*; Kay Boatner, *Assistant Editor*
Photo Kelley Miller, *Senior Editor*; Lisa Jewell, *Editor*
Art Eileen O'Tousa-Crowson, *Art Director*; Julide Obuz Dengel, *Designer*; Stephanie Rudig, *Digital Design Assistant*
Administration Bianca Bowman, *Editorial Assistant*; Tammi Colleary, *Business Specialist*
Production David V. Showers, *Director*
Proofreader Jane Sunderland
Online Anne A. McCormack, *Director*
International Magazine Publishing
Yulia Petrossian Boyle, *Senior Vice President*

STAFF FOR THIS BOOK
Erica Green, *Project Manager*
James Hiscott, Jr., *Art Director and Design*

MANUFACTURING AND QUALITY MANAGEMENT
Phillip L. Schlosser, *Senior Vice President, Production Services*
Chris Brown, *Vice President, NG Book Manufacturing*
Gregory Storer, *Director*
Robert L. Barr, *Manager*
Neal Edwards, *Imaging*

ROVIO ENTERTAINMENT LTD.
Pekka Laine, *Project Editor*
Mari Elomäki, *Project Editor*
Anna Makkonen, *Graphic Designer*

National Geographic's net proceeds support vital exploration, conservation, research, and education programs.

Copyright © 2013, 2014 National Geographic Society

© 2009–2014 Rovio Entertainment Ltd. Rovio, Angry Birds, Bad Piggies, Mighty Eagle, and all related properties, titles, logos, and characters are trademarks of Rovio Entertainment Ltd.

The content on pages 6-104 was previously published in the publication *Angry Birds: Explore the World!*, 2013.

Paperback ISBN: 978-1-4263-1810-8
Reinforced library binding ISBN: 978-1-4263-1987-7

Printed in the United States of America
14/WOR/1